"Why should we believe in God's unconditional election? First, because God has revealed it in his Word. Second, because God works through the doctrine of election to make his people like Christ. Joshua Banks has written a well-researched study that is rather unique because in it he argues for both the truth of the Reformed doctrine of election and its practical implications for worship, compassion, and evangelism. This is a model of academics done for the sake of the church."

—**Joel R. Beeke**, president, Puritan Reformed Theological Seminary, Grand Rapids, Michigan

"The biblical doctrine of election has been described as the Continental Divide of Christian theology because it profoundly impacts how we view ourselves and God. The resurgence of this doctrine in the last few decades has been heartening. However, one of the great deficiencies in this needed resurgence is the impact this glorious doctrine should have on the believer's sanctification. In many soteriologically reformed circles, there has been an intellectual embrace of election, but a neglect of the life-changing impact that should and necessarily follow this embrace upon our sanctification and personal holiness. If God's work in election is powerful enough to save us, then it is also powerful enough to transform us. I am so grateful for Joshua Banks' book, Yes, It Matters, because it not only provides a clear biblical defense of this essential doctrine, but also demonstrates how election must result in holy living to the glory of God. This book addresses one of the most glaring deficiencies that I and others have seen in Calvinistic circles, namely, a lack of sanctification. For this I am profoundly grateful and it is my absolute joy to commend Yes, It Matters to you. Do yourself a favor and read this important work."

—**Justin Peters**, founder of Justin Peters Ministries

"There are many theological paradigms to embrace. Josh's book presents this important paradigm: "theology drives methodology which leads to doxology." In other words, what you believe matters, even in matters of holy living and praise to the Father. Josh expertly guides the reader to the biblical fact that God elects and that election is tethered, practically, to holy living.

What people love in themselves, namely the ability to chose (spouses, friends, employment, food, sports' teams and more), they sometimes reject in God. Positively, since men and women are made in God's image, it should not surprise us that men and women like to choose, because God is sovereign and He chooses, elects and ordains! I heartily endorse Josh's work as he desires that the reader have a proper theology, methodology and ultimately doxology."

—**Mike Abendroth**, pastor of Bethlehem Bible Church
and host of No Compromise Radio

YES, IT MATTERS:

THE INFLUENCE OF THE DOCTRINE OF ELECTION ON SANCTIFICATION

JOSHUA B. BANKS

G³ Press

Yes, It Matters: The Influence of the Doctrine of Election on Sanctification

Copyright © 2022 by Joshua B. Banks

Published by G3 Press
4979 GA-5
Douglasville, GA 30135
www.G3Min.org

Printed in the United States of America by Graphic Response, Atlanta, GA.

ISBN: 978-0-9994317-8-8

Cover Design: Joe Zarate

To my lovely wife and children. Thank you for all your love and support throughout the time of writing this book. Second only to Christ, you are my greatest blessing from the Lord.

Contents

Foreword

First Thessalonians is one of the earliest—if not the earliest—of the inspired letters from the pen of the Apostle Paul. Written around the year ad 50, while Paul was ministering in Corinth on his second missionary journey (Acts 18:1-18), the letter begins with this thanksgiving:

> We give thanks to God always for all of you, making mention *of you* in our prayers; constantly bearing in mind your work of faith and labor of love and steadfastness of hope in our Lord Jesus Christ in the presence of our God and Father, knowing, brethren beloved by God, His choice of you. (1 Thess 1:2-4)

What is remarkable is how Paul refers to God's *choice* (ἐκλογή, *eklogē*, v. 4). At most, those to whom the apostle writes were a year old in the faith. Yet at this early stage of their lives as followers of Christ, Paul freely refers them to the doctrine of election. He adds no explanation or apology. He leaves no hint that the term would be controversial. Instead, he writes as though these new Thessalonian converts knew exactly what he was referring to. Moreover, in unusual and emphatic language, Paul joyously connects this term to a profound act of love. To say that these Thessalonians were the *chosen* or *elected of God* was the same as saying that they were *the beloved of God* (v. 4).

Sadly, the doctrine of election is not approached with the same simplicity and joy today as it was in the first century of the church. Among some Christians, the term is avoided altogether. The doctrine it describes is considered unnecessary to the Christian life and needlessly divisive. For others, the term may be accepted but substantially redefined, altering its meaning from an active, declarative sense to a far more passive idea. Instead of God's "choice" it becomes God's "acknowledgement." Still others maintain the term's original sense but limit its focus. God does not "choose" sinners to salvation, he only "chooses" the means by which sinners can be saved.

Those who reject the doctrine of God's sovereign, active choice of sinners unto salvation often argue that embracing such a doctrine undermines the pursuit of holiness. If you teach unconditional election—the argument goes—you will have no theological or logical basis upon which to press the imperatives of sanctification. You either teach election or sanctification, but you cannot do both—or so it is claimed.

Of course, nothing could be further from the truth. The Apostle Paul certainly saw no inconsistency between these doctrines. After thanking God for the election of the Thessalonian converts (1:2–4), Paul goes on to emphasize the imperatives of sanctification:

> Finally then, brethren, we request and exhort you in the Lord Jesus, that as you received from us *instruction* as to how you ought to walk and please God (just as you actually do walk), that you excel still more. For you know what commandments we gave you by *the authority of* the Lord Jesus. For this is the will of God, your sanctification. (1 Thess 4:1–3)

A considerable amount of the rest of 1 Thessalonians is then filled with imperatives. Clearly, Paul saw no contradiction. And even after he recorded all these exhortations to holiness from 4:1–5:22, he brings the letter to a close with another reference to the doctrine of sovereign choice. He first prays that God himself would bring the process of sanctification to its completion: "Now may the God of peace himself sanctify you entirely; and may your spirit and soul and body be preserved complete, without blame at the coming of our Lord Jesus Christ" (5:23). But he then states the promise so precious to all believers—one which is inextricably linked to the doctrine of unconditional election: "Faithful is he who calls you, and he will also bring it to pass" (v 24). Thus, Paul begins with election, and he closes with it.

This book by Joshua Banks that you hold in your hands emphasizes this same message: the doctrine of unconditional election is not incompatible with the doctrine of progressive sanctification. In fact, the two are necessarily related. It is the doctrine of election which empowers and ensures sanctification in all those who are truly saved. And sanctification is properly understood and pursued upon the basis of a right understanding of God's sovereignty in salvation. You cannot have one without the other. And when properly understood, the believer is given both powerful motivations and precious assurances. Therefore, if you are as serious about holiness and conformity to Jesus Christ as you should be, you should know and appreciate both of these doctrines and how they relate to one another.

This book will certainly help. It highlights and explains in short chapters the key issues and arguments involved in this crucial discussion. Moreover, it grounds its analysis and conclusions in the biblical text—not human logic, tradition, or intuition. To add to this, it is written with deep pastoral care. Joshua Banks writes not to insert himself into a heated theological debate. He writes because he cares deeply about the glory due Jesus Christ and about the well-being of souls.

If you are trying to work your way through these issues and need light, or if you already have but want to be encouraged, this book will help. I heartily recommend it because *yes, the doctrine of election matters to your growth in Christ.*

Brad Klassen
Associate Professor of Bible Exposition
The Master's Seminary

Preface

A common question asked today is, "What is God's will for my life," or "What does God desire of me?" The Scriptures answer these questions clearly. For example, God desires us to praise him (1 Pet 4:11), to be like him (Eph 5:1), to obey the Lord Jesus (John 14:15), to declare the gospel to the lost (Matt 28:19–20), and to walk humbly before the Lord (Jas 4:10). These are clear commands of the Lord in Scripture, and these would certainly be understood as the revealed will of God for the lives of His people. These commands, of which there are more, would not be disputed among believers.

However, the means of carrying out these commands are a matter of frequent debate among God's people. When believers are commanded to be compassionate, merciful, or gracious to unbelievers, what is the foundation on which believers are to cultivate these characteristics? When God says that he works all things for good to those who love God, upon what is that statement grounded and how is the comfort intended, realized, or appropriated? It is my conviction that the answer to these questions is the doctrine of election.

The doctrine of election is indeed a controversial topic among believers. It brings to the forefront subjects such as the atonement of Christ, the sovereignty of God, the providence of God, the love of God, salvation by grace alone, the depravity of man, freewill, and the workings of the Holy Spirit. This doctrine has been debated throughout church history and will no doubt continue to be debated in the years to come. The question most often presented is, "Why does it matter anyway what someone believes of election?" This is a genuine question, though often asked in attempt to silence the discussion. Why does it matter? What someone believes of the doctrine of election is not a salvation issue, so why even bring it up? When examining the texts of Scripture that deal with the doctrine of election, one will find that the teaching of election is not taught in a vacuum. In other words, there is something more that the authors of Scripture are teaching in light of the truth of election. The reason is that the doctrine of election has a direct impact on the life of the believer. Election is not simply an abstract or philosophical truth to marvel at or to debate over. This truth is to be experienced in God's people.

If the doctrine of election has been debated for years and years and will continue to be debated, then why am I writing a book on it? Of course, there are many books defending the Reformed doctrine of election and many books opposing it also. What makes this book different? This book isn't simply a book defending the Reformed view of election. This is a book that primarily explores the effects on the believer of having a right understanding of the doctrine of election. It is true that the Reformed view is emphasized throughout this study as being in agreement with Scripture. Again, the biblical writers had an intended result in mind when they wrote of this doctrine, and having a correct view is vitally important. The intended result would range from deepening the praise and adoration of God's people toward our King to grounding our Christian character in the reality of God's gracious election of His people. This study will briefly examine the subject of God's sovereignty to lay the necessary, biblical foundation of God's providence, and then briefly explore the primary views of election. In doing so, we will be able to see the implications of each view as to which one corresponds to the overall teaching of Scripture regarding God, Christ, salvation, and the spiritual condition of man.

This book is not intended to be an exhaustive study of God's sovereignty or the Reformed view of election. The primary focus is the effect of the biblical doctrine of election on the sanctification of God's people. There are specific aspects of God's sovereignty that will be discussed that will lead into the overall subject, but the main focus is the doctrine of election's influence on sanctification. Because there are various ideas of God's sovereignty, of what it means, and how His sovereign control is worked out in creation, there are two particular texts that will be considered to establish that God is intimately involved in every human decision, not just as a responder but as the initiator. Because of the various views of election also, some time needs to be spent looking at the different positions. The main views we encounter are the Corporate view, the Conditional, Individual view, and the Unconditional, Individual view, and these will be discussed in section two. Which one is correct? Which one agrees with the whole of Scripture concerning the nature and character of God, etc.? Once the necessary foundation of God's sovereignty and election is established, then we will move into the more practical section of the book, which explores the relationship between election and sanctification.

In section three, there are seven specific passages that are examined that deal with the relationship of election and sanctification. For example, the Apostle Paul, in one of the most often used texts to support the Reformed view of election, teaches that the truth of our Lord predestining His people unto salvation (election) is a comfort in the lives of the people of God (Rom 8:29–30). Paul also writes to the Ephesian believers about election in order to produce in them a genuine praise to God (Eph 1:4–7). This is true of many of the passages that teach of election. It is vital then to study the doctrine of election for the purpose of growth in all areas of the Christian life. The answer to the question, "Why does it matter anyway what someone believes of election?" is that it matters because it affects the believer's sanctification.

Abbreviations

BECNT	Baker Exegetical Commentary on the New Testament
BST	Bible Speaks Today
CC	Calvin's Commentaries
EBC	Expositor's Bible Commentary
ECNT	Exegetical Commentary on the New Testament
EGGNT	Exegetical Guide to the Greek New Testament
HNTC	Holman New Testament Commentary
LC	Lectio Continua Expository Commentary on the New Testament
MacNTC	MacArthur New Testament Commentary
NAC	New American Commentary
NASB	New American Standard Bible
NTC	New Testament Commentary
PNTC	Pillar New Testament Commentary
REC	Reformed Expository Commentary
TNTC	Tyndale New Testament Commentary

Section I

The Sovereignty of God

Chapter One
Divine Responder?

"To say that God is sovereign is to declare that he is the Almighty, the possessor of all power in heaven and earth, so that none can defeat his counsels, thwart his purposes, or resist his will."[1]

The Scriptures present us with a glorious reality that our God is above all gods. In fact, there are no other gods but him. Man may conjure up ideas in his mind of a god after his own liking, as man has done throughout the history of the world, but never do the imaginations of man ever compare to the reality of the majesty of the God who is. Our God, the only true God, has all power and authority in this world. He sees all things, is present everywhere at all times, and sustains all things by His mighty power. The Lord declares that the gods of people cannot see, hear, or smell (Deut 4:28). There are no other gods but him. What we think about God determines how we view and interpret various doctrines of Scripture, and how great or small we think he is. Though A. W. Tozer was not a Reformed theologian, what he states regarding our view of God is very much applicable to this study:

> What comes into our minds when we think about God is the most important thing about us. The history of mankind will probably show that no people has ever risen above its religion, and man's spiritual history will positively demonstrate that no religion has ever been greater than its idea of God. Worship is pure or base as the worshiper entertains high or low thoughts of God. For this reason the gravest question before the Church is always God himself, and the most portentous fact about any man is not what he at a given time may

---

[1] A. W. Pink, *The Sovereignty of God* (Carlisle, PA: Banner of Truth, 2009), 13.

say or do, but what he in his deep heart conceives God to be like. We tend by a secret law of the soul to move toward our mental image of God. This is true not only of the individual Christian, but of the company of Christians that composes the Church. Always the most revealing thing about the Church is her idea of God, just as her most significant message is what she says about him or leaves unsaid, for her silence is often more eloquent than her speech. She can never escape the self-disclosure of her witness concerning God.[2]

What we think of the Lord must be grounded in what we know and learn from the only authoritative source for God, which is the Holy Scripture. In the Scripture, truly, the Lord has revealed himself in order that our thoughts and knowledge of him would be true. This is vital for our understanding of the doctrine of election. The God whom we read of in Scripture is not a God under the sovereignty of man, but a God who is intimately sovereign over all things including the decisions and actions of men. The overall focus of this book is the practical implications of the doctrine of election, but those practical implications hinge on a correct understanding of God's sovereignty. If we are to cultivate the intended results of the doctrine of election in our sanctification, we must understand our God rightly.

Our Lord is the living God who is our only Sovereign. He is the Master—the Ruler of the heavens and earth—and God's rulership, His control, extends to everything; meaning, every event in the life of every human being, even down to every human decision is under God's sovereign control, in addition to everything else in existence. Derek Thomas says of God's sovereignty:

God is sovereign in creation, providence, redemption, and judgment. That is a central assertion of Christian belief and especially in Reformed theology. God is King and Lord of all. To put this another way: nothing happens without God's willing it to happen, willing it to happen before it happens, and willing it to happen in the way that it happens. Put this

---

[2] A. W. Tozer, *Knowledge of the Holy* (New York: Harper & Row, 1961), 1.

way, it seems to say something that is expressly Reformed in doctrine. But at its heart, it is saying nothing different from the assertion of the Nicene Creed: "I believe in God, the Father Almighty." To say that God is sovereign is to express His almightiness in every area.[3]

When we speak of God's sovereignty, we are not only speaking of God's right and power to do all that he decides to do, but also of His sovereign decrees and providence in all creation. God has decreed everything that comes to pass, and in the exercise of His decree in time and in history, he fulfills all His will perfectly so as no creature can hinder or thwart His will. Grudem states, "The decrees of God are the eternal plans of God whereby, before the creation of the world, he determined to bring about everything that happens."[4] In other words, God made sovereign decisions concerning everything before it was created. In time, he exercises His decisions sovereignly over all of creation and governs everything to that end, including all that occurs in the realm of humanity.

To be fair, the Arminian position of God's sovereignty claims that God is not simply idle in the events and circumstances in the history of humanity. Arminian Roger Olsen rejects that accusation saying, "God does not permit sin as a spectator; God is never in the spectator mode."[5] He goes on to state:

Classical Arminianism goes far beyond belief in general providence to include affirmation of God's intimate and direct involvement in every event of nature and history. The only thing the Arminian view of God's sovereignty necessarily excludes is God's authorship of sin and evil. Faithful followers of Arminius have always believed that God governs

---

[3] Derek Thomas, "God's Sovereignty and Our Responsibility," *Ligonier*, June 26, 2020, https://www.ligonier.org/posts/gods-sovereignty-and-our-responsibility.

[4] Wayne Grudem, *Systematic Theology* (Grand Rapids, MI: Inter-Varsity, 1994), 332

[5] Roger Olsen, *Arminian Theology: Myths and Realities* (Downers Grove: IVP, 2006), 122.

the entire universe and all of history. Nothing at all can happen without God's permission, and many things are specifically and directly controlled and caused by God. Even sin and evil do not escape God's providential governance in classical Arminian theology. God permits and limits them without willing or causing them.[6]

While these statements sound familiar, at least in part, to that of the Reformed tradition, the outworking of these statements are very different from what we find in Scripture concerning God's sovereignty and providence.

God's Power Exercised Over Creation

Both the Reformed and Arminian adherents speak of God's sovereignty, but how does each side view God's control over His creation, and specifically in the area of freewill and human decisions? How one answers this question will certainly demonstrate what one believes of predestination and salvation as a whole. Is God sovereign by right but not in actuality and therefore does not choose who will come to him, or is God absolutely in control over everything, including who will come to Christ? Did Jesus die for all people everywhere without distinction, or did he die for those the Father gave him only? Does the Holy Spirit equally effect the hearts of all people to repent, or does he regenerate the hearts of the elect, only enabling them to come to Christ? Lastly, can man come to Christ without the intervening work of God, or does he require the supernatural work of God to raise him to life in order to believe? It is necessary to flesh out what we mean and what the Arminian view means when it speaks of God's sovereignty.

Much of the debate about predestination centers around whether or not God is truly free to choose whom he will save, or if God saves those whom he knew would choose him by their own free choice. Simply put, who is the truly free agent, God or man? When we consider God's sovereign control over His creation, I

---

[6] Olsen, *Arminian Theology*, 116.

think it is vital to reflect upon the Scripture's description of God's sovereignty over everything. If God controls all things (weather, plants, animals, etc.) and holds the world together, then why would he not be sovereign over man and who receives His salvation? What kind of control does the Scripture present to us?

The Scripture teaches, of course, that God created all things and nothing came into being apart from him (Gen 1; John 1:3). God is over all and the above all things (John 3:31; Eph 4:6). Numerous passages teach us that God sends the rain, the hail, the lightning, the winds, etc. (Lev 26:3–4; Job 38:25–30; Ps 148:8). He has created the animals, feeds them, cares for them, uses them for His purposes, and ordains their end (Gen 1; 1 Kgs 17:2–6; Job 38:39–39:40; Ps 104:24–29; Dan 6:22; Jonah 1:17; Matt 6:26, 10:29, 17:22). Our Lord exercises His sovereign rule over the sun, moon, and stars (Gen 1:14–16; Josh 10:12–13; Job 38:31–33; Amos 5:8). Our Lord has created all things and sustains all things by His sovereign power (Col 1:16–17). Indeed, there are more passages than the ones listed above to express God's sovereignty over everything in existence. It is important to note that God's rule over all things is an active rule. He did not simply create and then allow everything to run as a clock. He actively participates in the care and rule over His creation. I stress this because when it comes to God's sovereign rule over man, irrespective of the claims by Arminians, God's role is understood mostly as a spectator role or a passive role rather than active.

God's Freedom or Man's Freedom?

If God is sovereign over everything else in existence, why would the realm of mankind be any different? This is the precise area, however, where much of the debate centers. For the Arminians, their main goal is to make certain that man has libertarian freewill and that God does not and will not violate that freewill. In Norman Geisler's book *Chosen But Free*, his reasoning and argumentation is based within the view that man has freewill and God does not violate it. In his attempt to justify his view by appealing to a number of church fathers, he states his view clearly:

"If affirming that God will not violate the free choice of any human being in order to save that person is an 'Arminian' view, then every major church father from the beginning . . . were Arminians!"[7] It is apparent that Geisler misrepresents the views of the early church fathers, and does so, perhaps, because the early church fathers, just like the apostles, believed in the free offer of the gospel to all people. Calvinists believe this also.

Dr. Geisler uses words like "predetermined" and "determined" and "sovereign" just as the Reformed camp would also, but the meanings of these words are very different and need to be defined. Dr. Geisler uses the word "determined" often in his book, but his meaning of this word carries the idea of a "passive" determining. Geisler's argumentation for the relationship of God's knowledge and determination is as follows:

1. God knows all things.

2. Whatever God foreknows must come to pass (i.e., is determined). If it did not come to pass, then God would have been wrong in what he foreknew. But an all-knowing Being cannot be wrong in what he foreknows.

3. God knew Judas would betray Christ.

4. Therefore, it *had to come to pass* (i.e., was determined) that Judas would betray Christ.[8]

Geisler uses the same reasoning when referring to salvation:

1. God knows all things.

2. Whatever God foreknows must come to pass (i.e., is predetermined).

3. God foreknew the Apostle John would accept Christ.

---

[7] Norman Geisler, *Chosen but Free* (Minneapolis: Bethany House, 2001), 53.
[8] Geisler, *Chosen but Free*, 42.

4. Therefore, it had to come to pass (as predetermined) that John would accept Christ.[9]

Dr. Geisler uses an interesting analogy to explain his position. He writes:

Let's again illustrate the harmony of predetermination and free choice. Suppose you cannot watch your favorite sports event live on TV. So you video tape it. When you watch it later, the entire game and every play in it are absolutely determined and can never be changed. No matter how many times you rerun it, the final score, as well as every aspect of every play, will always be the same. Yet when the fame happened, every event was freely chosen. No one was forced to play. Therefore, the same event was both determined and free at the same time.

Someone may object that this is so only because the event has already occurred, and that before the game occurred it was not predetermined. In response we need only point out that if God is all-knowing, then from the standpoint of His foreknowledge the game was predetermined. For *he* knew eternally exactly how it was going to turn out, even though we did not. Therefore, if God has infallible foreknowledge of the future, including our free acts, then everything that will happen in the future is predetermined, even our free acts. This does not mean these actions are not free; it simply means that God knew how we were going to use our freedom—and that he knew it *for sure*.[10]

In this reasoning, there is not an active determining of God. It is passive at best. He knows the future, and so he determined that it would be as he foreknew. In response, Dr. James White points out the fallacy of Geisler's reasoning:

---

[9] Geisler, *Chosen but Free*, 43.

[10] Geisler, *Chosen but Free*, 43.

It is important to follow this closely: God simply "knows" all of time and the free choices of humans that take place within time. God is not *determining* this actively, but passively. And this comes out in the final sentences: humans are "doing" things "freely." God "sees" what they are "freely doing." What God sees, he must know, and what he knows, he knows perfectly. Now, there is the key: "And what he knows, he determines." Knowing the free actions of men results in his "determining" those actions: passively, of course, not actively. This then is the meaning of "knowingly determining" what humans are "freely deciding."[11]

Dr. White points out that the decisions and decreeing are done by man and not by God. God is a responder to the decisions of man rather than him being the active determiner of everything.

Interestingly, this is basically what the staunch Arminian would say also, and yet Dr. Geisler critiques the staunch Arminian view saying, "If God's choice to save was based on those who choose him, then it would not be based on divine grace but would be based on human decisions. This flies in the face of the whole biblical teaching on grace."[12] This is certainly confusing to the reader because Geisler will go on to state his view, which he calls a moderate Calvinistic view:

> There is a third alternative. It postulates that God's election is neither based on His foreknowledge of man's free choices nor exercised independent of it. As the Scriptures declare, we are "elect according to the foreknowledge of God." That is to say, there is no chronological or logical priority of election and foreknowledge. . . . Both foreknowledge and predetermination are one in God. Whatever God knows, he determines. And whatever he determines, he knows. . . . God is totally sovereign in the sense of actually determining what occurs,

---

[11] James White, *The Potter's Freedom: A Defense of the Reformation and a Rebuttal to Norman Geisler's Chosen but Free* (Greenville, SC: Calvary Press Publishing, 2009) 52–53.

[12] Geisler, *Chosen but Free*, 50.

and yet man is completely free and responsible for what he chooses.[13]

What then is really the difference in Geisler's view and the staunch Arminian view? It has been understood that Geisler's view of God determining is passive and not active. It is also understood by his view that what God determines is based upon His knowledge. What God knows of future events, including the free choices of human beings, he determined that it would be as he knew it, and would make certain that it would come to pass. While the Arminian position would postulate that God looks down the corridor of time and elects whom he sees accepting Christ, Geisler would say that there is no chronological or logical priority of election because God sees all equally; because he's timeless and His fore-choosing and what he foreknows must be simultaneous, his view is still the same.

It is difficult to wrap my mind around Geisler's position and how it is truly different from the staunch Arminian position. If God knows all events and choices and determined that it would occur, then why would he need to intervene at all to bring it to pass? Why would God need to persuade anyone to come to Christ if in His knowledge of all human choices, he knew who would believe? Going back to his reasoning of the Apostle John's salvation: God is all-knowing; whatever God foreknows must come to pass (i.e., is predetermined); and God foreknew all who would believe. Therefore, it will have to come to pass (as predetermined) that all he knew would accept Christ will accept Christ. If God determined that everything he knows will come to pass as he knows it, then there shouldn't be any need for God to exercise any persuasion or power within the realm of mankind, unless one believes that God has to in order that His "determining" would not be thwarted.

Let's say for argument's sake that God's knowledge of who would believe was based upon His intervening work in their hearts. In other words, God knew that only certain ones would believe when, in His appointed time, he would "woo" them or

---

[13] Geisler, *Chosen but Free*, 52.

persuade them. Therefore, God knows with certainty that those he "foreknew" would believe, based on His persuading power, will come as a result of His intervention. If this is true, then what is the purpose of God granting the so-called prevenient grace to all? So that there are no misconceptions about this concept, one writer states, "Prevenient grace is grace that comes first. It precedes all human decision."[14] Roger Olsen writes that prevenient grace is "the illuminating, convicting, calling, and enabling power of the Holy Spirit working on the sinner's soul and making them free to choose saving grace (or reject it)."[15] Advocates of prevenient grace believe that through it the sinner is brought to a place of neutrality. In this state, the grace of God allows the sinner to have an enlightened knowledge of the gospel and the temporary ability to choose to believe if he desires.

In light of this understanding of prevenient grace, if God knows with certainty that only those he foreknew would be converted and come to Christ by His "wooing" and no others, then what is the point of granting prevenient grace to all? Why is it necessary for the Holy Spirit to attempt to persuade all when he knows with certainty only certain ones will come? It does not make any sense unless one believes that a person's "destiny" can change. Arminian Roger Olsen writes in agreement of William Pope's view of God's sovereignty:

> In good Arminian fashion Pope notes that God's providential governance of history necessarily includes the freewill of humans. His argument is that the very concept of providence or rulership loses much of its meaning if the objects of governance are subjected to "the unbending government of a soul that must act out its destiny." Rather, true government seeks to guide and persuade and teach, not control. "Hence, the most impressive view that may be taken of this doctrine regards it as the slow but sure guidance of all creatures whose

---

[14] Walter A. Elwell, *Evangelical Dictionary of Theology*, 2nd ed. (Grand Rapids: Baker Academic, 2001), 520.

[15] Roger Olsen, *Against Calvinism* (Grand Rapids: Zondervan, 2011), 67.

state is not yet eternally fixed to the consummation of their destiny as foreappointed of God."[16]

What does this imply? God guides, persuades, and teaches all His creatures that they might come to him, and that their eternal destiny, as foreknown by God, may change. With reasoning like this, it is no wonder that Olsen himself does not regard Open Theism as unorthodox. Open Theism is the logical conclusion to Arminianism!

The Never-Ending Dilemma

It is very apparent within the Arminian position that God is nothing more than the divine responder to mankind's freewill choices. The only thing that God has determined in the lives of believers regarding salvation is whatever he knew beforehand would occur. He knew who would believe and determined that what he knew would come to pass. This is the complete opposite of the Reformed view of God and His work in salvation. Though the Arminian position may consider these ideas to be more in protecting the character of God, the dilemma is still there regardless.

What I mean by this is that the dilemma of God choosing not to save all is still present. From the Arminian viewpoint, if God is all-knowing then he knew before he created anything that certain ones would choose him. He also knew all those who would not choose him, but he created them anyway. God created people knowing that they would have no hope of salvation. He created them knowing that their end would be destruction. The dilemma did not go away, but what does occur when the sovereignty of God is diminished is that the majesty of God is diminished—as well as the atonement—and the sovereignty of man is elevated to a status that doesn't belong to him. In the next chapter we will examine two texts of Scripture that will demonstrate that God is

---

[16] Olsen, *Arminian Theology*, 131.

not a responder to man, but rather that man is a responder to God.

Questions for Reflection

1. Do you view God as being sovereign over everything without exception?
2. Does God have the right to do as he pleases in heaven and on the earth?
3. Does man have greater freewill than God?
4. Does God simply know what will happen in the future or does he actively decide the future?
5. Do you acknowledge that God does not intend to save all?

Chapter Two
Sovereignty and Freewill

"God so presents the outside inducements that man acts in accordance with his own nature, yet does exactly what God has planned for him to do."[1]

Inevitably, when we emphasize God's sovereignty, it is only a matter of time before the issue of man's freewill arises. How do these seemingly opposite concepts go together? Ultimately, these concepts are reconciled within the infinite mind of God, however, there are certain aspects of the two realities that we can learn and know from Scripture. The desire of all should be that the glory of God is not diminished at all by our conclusions in this matter. Since the Scriptures are the final authority, then it is vital that we rely on its teaching and not our own subjective or emotional feelings. Emotional feelings, in my opinion, are what drives much of the opposition against the Reformed view. I say this because the Scriptures are very clear on the nature of God's sovereignty, especially, in the realm of salvation, and yet, many still refuse to concede to its truth. I have personally heard some Christians say, "But my God isn't like that. He wouldn't choose some and not others." Statements like these have a profound effect on our view of God as a whole, and inevitably places man in the seat of authority over his salvation.

This is the very problem that is the focus of this study. If man believes himself to be the final authority in his salvation, then his appreciation and gratefulness to God for that salvation is not what it ought to be, and hence, his sanctification is affected, and, to some extent, hindered. As we enter into this weighty subject

---

[1] Loraine Boettner, *The Reformed Doctrine of Predestination* (Grand Rapids: Eerdmans, 1951), 38.

of God's sovereignty and man's freewill, we will begin with looking at the Arminian view.

A Limited God?

How do God's sovereignty and freewill cooperate together according to the Arminian view? The cooperation occurs by means of "God's self-limitation," a concept propagated within Arminian Theology. What does this mean? Again, Olsen writes of this idea by Arminian theologians:

> But they (Arminians) sought to develop a concept of God's sovereignty that would avoid making God the author of sin and evil, something they believed Calvinism could not do. This necessarily involved the idea of God's voluntary self-limitation in relation to creation for the sake of human liberty. They believed that this does not detract from God's sovereign oversight of human decisions and actions; thus God is able to make everything work together for good in his plan and purpose. Above all, these Arminians affirmed that nothing can happen apart from God's permission. God is sufficiently powerful to stop anything from happening, but he does not always exercise that power, because to do so would be to rob his free and rational creatures, created in his image, of their distinct reality and liberty.[2]

As Olsen stated, this concept was developed by the Arminian camp. It was not a concept that one would find within Scripture. For the Arminian, God cannot be in control over every action within the realm of humanity, such as the Fall or other sinful acts of man, because in their view, God would be held responsible for those circumstances. Rather, God uses the sinful actions of man and can bring good out of it; ultimately, he will guide everything to fulfill His purposes. Truly, God does bring good out of sinful

---

[2] Olsen, *Arminian Theology*, 132

actions or circumstances, but, again, God is not simply respond-ing to the decisions of man. God's role is much more than this. It is not that God's role is to limit himself and influence man when necessary to maintain His purposes and guide him to His in-tended end of things. God is the Planner! He is the Initiator! He is the Power behind everything that occurs in this world!

In God's sovereign decree he brings to pass all he desires, and none can thwart His will. The most significant event in history was the crucifixion of our Lord Jesus. We read in the gospels of the arrest of Christ, the mock trial, the slander and beating he endured, the mocking of King Herod and his approval of Christ's arrest and trial, the scourging from Pilate and the trial by the Ro-mans, the crowds calling for His death, and the crucifixion. In view of all of those things and more, the Scripture states in Acts 4:27–28, "For truly in this city there were gathered together against Your holy servant Jesus, whom You anointed, both Herod and Pontius Pilate, along with the Gentiles and the peoples of Is-rael, to do whatever Your hand and Your purpose predestined to occur." The apostles are giving all the credit to the Lord for all the events that took place surrounding Christ's death. Interestingly, Peter also does not diminish the responsibility of the people in the event in Acts 2:23: "this Man, delivered over by the predeter-mined plan and foreknowledge of God, you nailed to a cross by the hands of godless men and put him to death." How do these concepts go together? This will move us into the subject of con-currence.

Concurrence

The relationship of God's active control in man and man's re-sponsibility lead us into the subject of concurrence. In speaking of the subject of concurrence, MacArthur and Mayhue express this truth:

God's concurrence is his operation with created things, caus-ing them (whether acting directly or ordaining them through secondary causes), through their properties, to act. Examples in Scripture abound. Joseph said that God, not his brothers, sent him to Egypt. The Lord (Yahweh) said that he would be with Moses's mouth to enable him to speak for God. The Lord promised to deliver the enemies of Joshua and the people of Israel—the Israelites still had to attack, but the Lord gave them a great victory. God turns a king's heart to do as God wills, and the Lord turned the heart of the king of Assyria to help the people in building the temple. The Lord gave the people of Israel the ability to acquire wealth. God works in believers "to will and to work for his good pleasure." God has ordered evil acts, such as when he moved Shimei to curse David. He used Assyria to chastise his people. He "put" a lying spirit in the mouths of Ahab's prophets.[3]

According to the above references in Scripture, it is God who was actively controlling each of those events and more. The Arminian camp would staunchly disagree as we read from Olsen. The Fall and other acts of evil cannot be within the sovereign decree of God, but this is precisely what we understand from Scripture. For example, all that occurred in Egypt when the children of Israel were in bondage happened because it was in accordance with God's sovereign will. We read in Romans 9:17 that the Lord raised up Pharaoh in order to demonstrate His power in him. Again, the emphasis is that the Lord raised him up.

How does all this work together? Do we resort to diminishing God's power and sovereign providence to grant the creature more freedom that what he actually has? This is certainly what the Arminian position does. Its sole focus is on the liberty of the creature rather than the freedom of the Creator to do as he wills. Roger Olsen demonstrates this as he states, "According to [Arminius's view of divine concurrence], God does not permit sin as a spectator; God is never in the spectator mode. Rather, God not only allows sin and evil designedly and willingly, although not approvingly or efficaciously, but he cooperates with the creature

---

[3] John MacArthur and Richard Mayhue, *Biblical Doctrine: A Systematic Summary of Biblical Truth* (Wheaton: Crossway, 2017), 220.

in sinning without being stained by the guilt of sin."[4] Olsen goes on to state:

> Once God decides to permit an act, even a sinful one, he can-not consistently withhold the power to commit it. However, in the case of sinful or evil acts, whereas the same event is produced by both God and the human being, the guilt of the sin is not transferred to God, because God is the effecter of the act but only the permitter of the sin itself. This is why Scripture sometimes attributes evil deeds to God; because God concurs with them. God cooperates with the sinners who commit them. But that does not mean God is the efficacious cause of them or wills them. . . . God allows them and cooper-ates with them unwillingly in order to preserve the sinners' liberty, without which sinners would not be responsible and repentant persons would not enter into a truly personal and loving relationship with God.[5]

What does Olsen mean by these words? It seems that he is saying that God is not simply a spectator, because it is God who allows the act and provides the sinner the ability to carry out his evil. He states very clearly, though, that God has not willed the act nor is he the efficacious cause. He also implies that God is an unwill-ing participant, but does so in order to preserve the sinners' lib-erty. The question is, however, what truth do the Scriptures pre-sent to us concerning God's role in the decisions of man and his carrying out his sinful deeds?

Before considering two specific passages, it is critical to note that nowhere in Scripture does God ever act wickedly, or ever take pleasure in evil. He is never shown to have directly done any evil. He is altogether righteous and holy and there is no darkness in him. Man is absolutely responsible for his actions and is righty held accountable, and yet at the same time, man does exactly what God intended for him to do. We find in Scripture that God has indirectly brought about certain evil acts through people or

---

[4] Olsen, *Arminian Theology*, 122.

[5] Olsen, *Arminian Theology*, 122–23

even Satan and his demons. One of the most popular texts to express the biblical view of divine concurrence occurs in the life of Joseph and Pharaoh. It is these two events which will be discussed further.

God, the Power Behind Human Decisions

It is in the account of Joseph that we find that God did more than allow an evil act to occur, but rather he caused this evil act to occur. Grudem writes, "Scripture clearly says that Joseph's brothers were wrongly jealous of him (Gen 37:11), hated him (Gen 37:4, 5, 8), wanted to kill him (Gen 37:20), and did wrong when they cast him into a pit (Gen 37:24), and then sold him into slavery (Gen 37:28). Yet later Joseph could say to his brothers, 'God sent me before you to preserve life' (Gen 45:5), and, 'You meant evil against me; but God meant it for good, to bring it about that many people should be kept alive, as they are today' (Gen 50:20)."[6] Joseph's brothers had no idea that they were fulfilling exactly what God intended for them to do, and yet they accomplished God's purposes, though their intent was evil. It was through the wickedness of Joseph's brothers that God brought about the salvation of those in Egypt during the famine. In this instance, God was using secondary means to accomplish His will. Derek Thomas writes:

> God is the "first cause" of all things, but evil is a product of "secondary causes." In the words of John Calvin, "First, it must be observed that the will of God is the cause of all things that happen in the world: and yet God is not the author of evil," adding, "for the proximate cause is one thing, and the remote cause another." In other words, God himself cannot do evil and cannot be blamed for evil even though it is part of His sovereign decree.[7]

---

[6] Grudem, *Systematic Theology*, 323.

[7] Thomas, "God's Sovereignty and Our Responsibility."

God had decreed for Joseph to be sent to Egypt, and God decreed the means of how he would get there. This was God's plan and His doing. The psalmist as he recounts God's dealings with His people writes of this in Psalm 105:17: "He sent a man before them, Joseph, who was sold as a slave." God did not see this event occurring and decide then to bring about some good from it; rather he planned this event, and it occurred because it was His will for it to occur, which includes the actions of Joseph's brothers. MacArthur and Mayhue state:

> God does more than simply give the energy to second causes to do something; he directs the actions of second causes to his intended end. In this way, God, not man, is in control.... This concurrence is not a cooperative synergism, which would involve partial participation by both God and man. Rather, both are entirely engaged in causing this action. God's will is ultimately behind the act, and he provides the energy. But man as the second cause initiates the action in time, in response to God's direct causation or in response to man's own desires as stimulated by circumstances. The concurrence is initiated by God, and he has the priority in the action, or else man would be independently sovereign in his actions. God's concurrence is logically prior to human action and predetermines everything outside God. The arrangement is never that man initiates an act and that God joins in after the initiation. God provides not energy in general but actual energy to do specific acts in his decree.[8]

In contrast to Olsen and Arminius, MacArthur and Mayhue point out that God is not a responder to man's decision to perform an evil action, but rather God actively initiates the desire for the action. Man's actions are in direct agreement with the decreed will of God. "Man never works independently of God in anything. God always accompanies man with his (God's) effectual will, yet without coercing man to violate his nature in any act."[9] In other

---

[8] MacArthur and Mayhue, *Biblical Doctrine*, 220–221.
[9] MacArthur and Mayhue, *Biblical Doctrine*, 221.

words, man is only sinful. He is born with a sinful nature, he desires to sin, and as Jesus said, "Men loved the darkness rather than light" (Jn 3:19). When God directly or indirectly brings about a certain evil action through a sinful human being, he is not having to coerce them to do it. They are sinful already and they want to carry out wickedness. The actions that he purposes for them to carry out is exactly consistent with their natures.

Another example of this is Pharaoh during the time of the Exodus. In the book of Exodus we read in chapter 4:21: "But I (the Lord) will harden his (Pharaoh's) heart so that he will not let the people go." This is repeated again in 7:3, 9:12, 10:1, 10:20, 10:27, 11:10, 14:4, and 14:8. We also read that Pharaoh hardened his own heart: 8:15, 8:32, and 9:34. This is a great source of debate between Reformed and Arminian believers. How are we to understand this working of God? Answer—in the same manner as we understood the circumstance with Joseph and his brothers. The Lord says to Moses in Exodus 7:3, "But I will harden Pharaoh's heart that I may multiply My signs and My wonders in the land of Egypt." This was a promise by the Lord, and the purpose of God's hardening of Pharaoh's heart was to show His glory and power.

This was an action performed by God and not simply God foreseeing this action by Pharaoh, or as Jack Cottrell writes that God only influences the person by placing certain thoughts into their minds. He says of God working this in certain individuals:

God works through special providence . . . by directly planting certain thoughts and mental states into the minds of individuals. For example, God can instill within people's hearts either the attitude of favor toward others (Gen 39:21; Exod 12:36), or the attitude of fear (Exod 23:27; Deut 2:25). Also, I believe that we must grant that God can cause certain memories to arise or certain thoughts to be present in a person's consciousness. We usually think of Satan as doing this very thing as a means of temptation (e. g. John 13:2). If this is possible for Satan, surely it is possible for God. Once these thoughts or memories are present in the mind, they become the occasion for making decisions of one kind or another.

These decisions are ours to make, but they may be influenced by the thoughts.[10]

So according to Cottrell's view, the Lord just puts a thought into the mind of the person to influence them to do what he desires, while the decision is still theirs to make. When speaking of Pharaoh specifically, he writes:

> It is possible that God hardened Pharaoh's heart in a similar manner. Via divine intervention certain thoughts may have flooded his mind, e.g., what a great loss of free labor it would be to lose these Israelites, or what a laughingstock he would be when other nations heard how a bunch of slaves bested him. God could have made sure that Pharaoh would think of these things at just the appropriate time, i.e., when he was weakening and about to let the people go.[11]

He comments that God is not violating anyone's freewill by performing this act because God is not causing anyone to do anything, but rather seeking to influence a decision; he then also states, "Sometimes the desired decision is not made."[12] This he stated in reference to the Lord sending droughts and famines upon His people in Amos 4:6–11 and Haggai 1:1–11 and the people still not responding to him.

Norman Geisler comments on the Exodus passages referencing the hardening of Pharaoh's heart:

> God did not harden Pharaoh's heart contrary to Pharaoh's own free choice. The Scriptures make it very clear that Pharaoh hardened his own heart. They declare that Pharaoh's heart "grew hard" (Exod 7:13; cf. 7:14, 22), that Pharaoh "hardened his heart" (Exod 8:15), and that "Pharaoh's heart grew hard" the more God worked on it (8:19 NKJV). Again, when God sent the plagues of the flies, "Pharaoh hardened

---

[10] Jack Cottrell, *The Faith Once for All* (Joplin, MO: College Press Publishing, 2002), 124.

[11] Cottrell, *The Faith Once for All*, 124.

[12] Cottrell, *The Faith Once for All*, 124.

his heart at this time also heart at this time also" (8:32 NKJV). This same phrase, or like phrases, are repeated over and over. While it is true that God predicted in advance that it would happen (Exod 4:21), nonetheless the fact is that Pharaoh hardened his own heart first (7:13; 8:15, etc.) and then God only hardened it later (cf. 9:12; 10:1, 20, 27). Further, it was God's mercy that occasioned the hardening of Pharaoh's heart. For each time he pleaded with Moses to lift the plague, he was further confirmed in his sin by adding to his guilt and by making it easier for him to reject God the next time.[13]

In other words, God knew what Pharaoh would do in advance and only acted upon Pharaoh's heart after Pharaoh hardened his own heart first. Again, the Lord is nothing more than a responder to the decisions of man. He only acts after the individual has acted first.

What do the above ideas and views imply about the Lord? A few of these implied ideas from the views of Geisler and Olsen include the following several statements. First, God is not exercising any true sovereign control over these situations. He only knows what will occur and when it happens that Pharaoh hardens his heart, it is only then the Lord hardens his heart. Second, God's control is passive; meaning, His power is limited and he only places certain thoughts into the minds of individuals to influence them to do what he desires. However, according to the Arminian view, this does not always work. The overall implication is God's knowledge is elevated above His omnipotence, and, once again, God is only a responder rather than the sovereign initiator and planner. The glory of God as demonstrated in His sovereign, active control is diminished in order that man may have freewill.

---

[13] Geisler, *Chosen but Free*, 90.

God's Glorious Purposes

Instead of finding ways to explain away the fact that the Lord planned to harden Pharaoh's heart before Moses ever went before him, and at least ten times we are told that it was the Lord who hardened it, we should seek to ask why the Lord did it. The Lord says to Moses in Exodus 4:21, "'When you go back to Egypt see that you perform before Pharaoh all the wonders which I have put in your power; but I will harden his heart so that he will not let the people go.'" Could it have been that if the Lord had not hardened his heart that Pharaoh would have let the people go during Moses's first encounter with him? It would seem so, otherwise, the Lord would not have had to intervene. The Lord actively hardened his heart so that he would not let them go and Moses would perform the signs commanded by the Lord. In Exodus 10:1–2 the Lord says to Moses:

> Go to Pharaoh, for I have hardened his heart and the heart of his servants, that I may perform these signs of Mine among them, and that you may tell in the hearing of your son, and of your grandson, how I made a mockery of the Egyptians and how I performed My signs among them, that you may know that I am the Lord.

The Lord hardened the heart of Pharaoh and made certain that he would not let the people of God go so that the Lord would demonstrate His power through the signs and wonders he would accomplish in Egypt. John Piper writes, "The Lord hardens Pharaoh so that he may multiply his wonders. He multiplies his wonders to put Pharaoh in his place, show the Egyptians that he is the absolute Lord, establish himself as the center of Israel's worship for generations, and make a name for himself in all the earth."[14]

The Apostle Paul records God's purpose in raising up Pharaoh being for the purpose of demonstrating His power in him. Romans 9:17 states, "For the Scripture says to Pharaoh, 'For this

---

[14] John Piper, *Providence* (Wheaton: Crossway, 2020), 437.

very purpose I raised you up, to demonstrate My power in you, and that My name might be proclaimed throughout the whole earth.'" This quote comes from Exodus 9:16 from the LXX, though there are some differences between the Greek rendition in Romans 9 and the LXX. Schreiner comments on these differences:

> Three significant differences from the LXX are found in Rom. 9:17. (1) The words *eis auto touto* (for this reason) are used instead of *kai heneken toutou* (and on account of this) and intensify the purpose for which Pharaoh was raised up. (2) The verb *exēgeira* (I raised up) replaces the verb *dieterethēs* (you have been preserved). Some scholars say that the LXX captures the MT better than Paul does, for they understand Exod. 9:16 to say that Pharaoh's life was preserved for the purpose articulated. Paul uses the verb "I raised you up" (*exēgeira*) to emphasize that Pharaoh's appearance in history was in accordance with and determined by God's will. Actually, Paul's translation may represent the sense of the Hebrew (he '*ēmadtīkā*, I have made you stand) better than the LXX and reflect God's sovereignty in establishing what occurs in the world. (3) The noun *dynamin* (power) is used instead of *ischyn* (power), and some commentators suggest that Paul prefers *dynamin* since it accords with the saving power of the gospel expressed in Rom. 1:16.[15]

As Schreiner points out, the Apostle Paul's use of the different wording is to emphasize God's sovereign action in raising Pharaoh up for the purpose of making His name great. Schreiner goes on to state, "From the 'raising up' of Pharaoh, Paul concludes that God 'hardens' whom he wills. These words confirm that Pharaoh was raised up by God for judgement. A careful analysis of the OT text also reveals that God's hardening of Pharaoh precedes and undergirds Pharaoh's self-hardening, and it is an imposition on the text to conclude that God's hardening is a response to the

---

[15] Thomas R. Schreiner, *Romans*, BECNT, 2nd ed. (Grand Rapids: Baker Academic, 1998), 814. (Emphasis mine).

hardening of human beings."[16] In other words, both Moses's and the Apostle Paul's intent is to demonstrate that God planned and performed this act upon Pharaoh, not as a response to Pharaoh but as the divine, active Agent. Pharaoh's action of hardening his heart was the effect of God already hardening his heart.

While passages like the above texts are explained in such a way that the plain meaning of the Scripture is ignored, the passages clearly express the reality of God actively performing all of His will and purposes in the lives of those he created. God is not passive but very active to be sure. God has the freedom to do as he pleases in heaven and on earth. As the Apostle Paul says, "He has mercy upon whom he desires and hardens whom he desires" (Rom 9:18). John Piper comments:

> God makes the choice to treat one with mercy and one with hardening unconditionally. Nothing in any person provides a criterion for one being hardened and another receiving mercy. The distinction lies in the will of God. The distinction lies not in man. Yet those who are hardened are truly guilty and truly deserve judgement for the rebellious condition of their hearts. Their own consciences will justly condemn them. If they perish, they will perish for real sin and real guilt. How God freely hardens and yet preserves human accountability, we are not told.[17]

We are to accept the plain meaning of Scripture even though we cannot comprehend how the two seemingly opposite ideas are both true. It is truly a mystery, but it is never the answer to diminish the majesty of God to preserve liberty in humanity. There are indeed many great mysteries in Scripture that our finite minds cannot comprehend, such as the Triune nature of God and the incarnation. We accept what the Scripture teaches us rather than coming up with new ideas to reconcile the irreconcilable.

There are many other passages that one can examine that teach the same as the above Scriptures. For example, the Lord

---

[16] Schreiner, *Romans*, 816.

[17] Piper, *Providence*, 443–44.

sends a lying spirit into the mouths of the prophets of Baal to entice Ahab to war (1 Kgs 22:19–23), and the text tells us plainly, "Now therefore, behold, the Lord has put a deceiving spirit in the mouth of all these your prophets; and the Lord has proclaimed disaster against you" (1 Kgs 22:23). We are also told in Acts 4:27–28 that Herod, Pontius Pilate, the Gentiles, and the people of Israel did what God predestined them to do when it came to the arrest, trial, condemnation, and crucifixion of the Lord Jesus Christ. All of this presents us with the reality that God actively performs what he purposes to occur in this world. He is sovereign over every aspect of His creation, from the sun, moon, stars, the universe, to the plants, animals, natural disasters, and down to the very decisions and actions of mankind.

The Lord is never a responder to the will of man. The Lord's plan and purposes are not brought about by what he knows in advance that man will do. There is no limitation to how the Lord carries out His will in this world. There is nowhere in Scripture that we are ever taught that God has limited His active power. Instead, we find passages like these:

> Blessed be the Lord, the God of our fathers, who has put such a thing as this in the king's heart, to adorn the house of the Lord which is in Jerusalem. (Ezra 7:27)

> The Lord has established His throne in the heavens, and His sovereignty rules over all. (Ps 103:19)

> But our God is in the heavens; he does whatever he pleases. (Ps 115:3)

> Whatever the Lord pleases, he does, in the host of heaven and in earth, in the seas and in all the deeps. (Ps 135:6)

> The Lord has made everything for its own purpose, even the wicked for the day of evil. (Prov 16:4)

> Many plans are in a man's heart, but the counsel of the Lord will stand. (Prov 19:21)

The king's heart is like channels of water in the hand of the Lord; he turns it wherever he wishes. (Prov 21:1)

Declaring the end from the beginning, and from ancient times things which have not been done, saying, 'My purpose will be established, and I will accomplish all My good pleasure'; calling a bird of prey from the east, the man of My purpose from a far country. Truly I have spoken; truly I will bring it to pass. I have planned it, surely I will do it. (Isa 46:10–11)

The Lord gave Jehoiakim king of Judah into his [Nebuchadnezzar] hand. (Dan 1:2)

I blessed the Most High and praised and honored him who lives forever; for His dominion is an everlasting dominion, and His kingdom endures from generation to generation. All the inhabitants of the earth are accounted as nothing. But he does according to His will in the host of heaven and among the inhabitants of the earth; and no one can ward off His hand or say to him, "what have You done?" (Dan 4:34–35)

And he made from one man every nation of mankind to live on the face of the earth, having determined their appointed times and the boundaries of their habitation, that they would seek God, if perhaps they might grope for him and find him, though he is not far from each one of us; for in him we live and move and exist. (Acts 17:26–28)

Of course, there are more Scriptures that express these same truths about God's active role and power in this world.

The reality that we find over and over again in Scripture is God is sovereign by right and sovereign in actuality. There are no limitations for him. He knows the future, not simply because he has perfect knowledge of all events and decisions, but he planned the future and carries out all His will. He actively brings about all that he desires in the decisions of man, and yet man, is still guilty for his own sinful actions, though he did exactly what God determined to occur. God's sovereignty extends to every part of the life of individuals, especially in the realm of salvation, which will be discussed in the next section.

Questions for Reflection

1. Has God limited himself with respect to man?
2. Is man able to thwart the will of God at any point?
3. Though God does not approve of sin, does he decree its existence?

4. Do you agree that Pharaoh's hardening of his own heart was a response to God's hardening?
5. Do you agree that God's rule over man is an active rule rather than a passive rule?

Section II

Understanding Election

Chapter Three
Various Views of the Doctrine of Election

"If we are to be biblical . . . the issue is not whether we should have a doctrine of predestination or not, but what kind we should embrace."[1]

This section will examine the various views of the doctrine of election and give a summary of each. This isn't intended to be an exhaustive study as there are many books that discuss the doctrine of election in much more detail. Because there are various views of this doctrine, the focus of section two is to establish what this writer believes to be the biblical teaching before heading into election's influence on sanctification. For some, election is the corporate view whereby God does not choose individuals, but chose Christ Jesus in whom are all who believe. As a result of belief in Christ, the Chosen One, believers are counted as the elect in him. For others, election is individual whereby God knows in advance those who will believe, and on that basis, he elects them to faith. I myself hold to the third view of election, often called the "Reformed" view, namely, as stated by Wayne Grudem: election "is an act of God before creation in which he chooses some people to be saved, not on account of any foreseen merit in them, but only because of His sovereign good pleasure."[2]

What is Election?

Though this is not an in-depth study, this doctrine permeates this entire book, and, therefore, defining the teaching of election

---

[1] R. C. Sproul, *Chosen by God* (Wheaton: Tyndale House, 1986), 11.
[2] Grudem, *Systematic Theology*, 670.

is vital to the overall thesis, which is election's influence on sanctification. Simply put, election is God choosing to save some out of the entire human race, and pass over others and allow them their due justice. In this statement, we have a few different concepts that need to be understood: predestination, election, and reprobation. The first is "predestination." The term predestination "concerns God's decision to elect some to salvation (election) and His decision to pass over others and punish them for their sins (reprobation)."[3] The concepts of election and predestination are indeed similar; however, there are slight observable differences to note between them:

> The term predestination is often employed as a synonym for God's decree, since he predestines all things. However, it is also used more narrowly to summarize God's dealings with fallen man concerning salvation, and in that sense it has a twofold meaning: the doctrine of predestination concerns God's decision to elect some to salvation and His decision to pass over others and punish them for their sins.[4]

Therefore, predestination means, "God's eternal, uninfluenced determination of all things; specifically, God's eternal choice of those who will be saved and those who will be passed over and condemned for their sin."[5] In other words, predestination refers to God's determination of the destinies of all people whether elect or reprobate. Election is the positive aspect of predestination and concerns those whom the Lord chose to be recipients of His unmerited grace. For example, the Apostle Paul writes in Ephesians 1:5, "He predestined us to adoption as sons through Jesus Christ to himself, according to the kind intention of His will." The apostle also uses this word in Romans 8:29–30 of the recipients of His saving grace: "For those whom he foreknew, he also predestined to become conformed to the image of His Son, so that he would be the firstborn among many brethren; and these

---

[3] MacArthur and Mayhue, *Biblical Doctrine*, 493.

[4] MacArthur and Mayhue, *Biblical Doctrine*, 493.

[5] MacArthur and Mayhue, *Biblical Doctrine*, 935.

whom he predestined, he also called; and these whom he called, he also justified; and these whom he justified, he also glorified." In these texts, God's predestination of individuals is positive: they are adopted and are sanctified, called, justified, and glorified.

As seen in the above paragraph, election is the positive side of God predestinating individuals to save, and reprobation would be the negative side. This particular teaching does indeed cause many disputes, but it needs to be understood that there are differences between election and reprobation. Reprobation is an aspect of predestination and concerns those from whom the Lord chose to withhold His grace. Reprobation could be described as the opposite side of the coin from election, though not quite. Reformed theologians call the relationship between election and reprobation "asymmetrical." In other words, they are not the exact same kind of acts, one just positive, and one just negative. Reprobation "is the free and sovereign choice of God, made in eternity past, to pass over certain individuals, choosing not to set His saving love on them but instead determining to punish them for their sins unto the magnification of His justice."[6] Berkhof defines reprobation as "that eternal decree of God whereby he has determined to pass some men by with the operations of His special grace, and to punish them for their sins, to the manifestation of His justice."[7] R. C. Sproul writes that predestination is double, and goes on to state, "Double predestination is unavoidable if we take Scripture seriously."[8] It is double in that it pertains to both the elect and the reprobate, but this double predestination is not symmetrical.

It is apparent from Scripture that God did not intend to save all human beings from their depravity and its consequences, but rather that God intended to save some and to pass over the rest. Jude 4 states, "For certain persons have crept in unnoticed, those who were long beforehand marked out for this condemnation,

---

[6] MacArthur and Mayhue, *Biblical Doctrine*, 504.

[7] Louis Berkhof, *Systematic Theology* (Grand Rapids: Eerdmans, 1996), 116.

[8] R. C. Sproul, *Essential Truths of the Christian Faith* (Carol Stream, IL: Tyndale House, 1992), 173.

ungodly persons who turn the grace of our God into licentious-
ness and deny our only Master and Lord, Jesus Christ." In 1 Peter
2:8 the apostle writes, "'and, a stone of stumbling and a rock of
offense'; for they stumble because they are disobedient to the
word, and to this doom they were also appointed." There is an
important distinction to be made between election and reprobation, and that is election is an active work of God and reprobation
is passive. Grudem again writes, "In the presentation of Scripture the cause of election lies in God, and the cause of reprobation
lies in the sinner. Another important difference is that the
ground of election is God's grace, whereas the ground of reprobation is God's justice."[9] Sproul states that "in the case of the reprobate he does not work evil in them or prevent them from coming to faith. Rather, he passes over them, leaving them to their
own sinful devices."[10] The reprobate are passed over while the
elect are graciously and actively brought to faith. MacArthur and
Mayhue write, "Just as God has *determined* the eternal destiny of
those sinners who will eventually be saved, so also has he *determined* the destiny of those sinners who will eventually be lost.
The former is the decree of election; the latter is the decree of
reprobation."[11] These things are important to note because one of
the charges against the Reformed position is that in reprobation
God actively hardens the sinner that he cannot come if he wanted
to. The picture some paint is of a person who wants to be saved
but God will not let them because he is chosen to endure God's
justice. This kind of person doesn't exist. The unregenerate will
never want to come to Christ. This will be discussed later. However, if we understand this doctrine correctly, we will see that
election and reprobation are not identical as the above statements demonstrate. One is active (election), and the other is passive (reprobation).

The above view of election is considered to be unconditional;
meaning, there was nothing in the creature, merit or foreseen

---

[9] Grudem, *Systematic Theology*, 686.

[10] Sproul, *Essential Truths of the Christian Faith*, 174.

[11] MacArthur and Mayhue, *Biblical Doctrine*, 504. Emphasis mine.

faith, upon which God based His election of them.[12] This is vitally important to understand because the writers of Scripture state that salvation is a gift of pure grace. The Lord's statement to the people of Israel in Deuteronomy 7:7-8 is an example of the Lord's choice of one nation over another. Though this passage is used by adherents of the corporate view as a proof of their position, it nonetheless proves that the Lord chose to enter into relationship with Israel and not any other nation. In doing so, there was not any injustice with God, but rather he decided to have mercy on Israel and make only them the objects of His special love. The Lord stated, "The Lord did not set His love on you nor choose you because you were more in number than any of the peoples, for you were fewest of all peoples, but because the Lord loved you and kept the oath which he swore to your forefathers, the Lord brought you out by a mighty hand and redeemed you from the house of slavery, from the hand of the Pharaoh, king of Egypt" (Deut 7:7-8). The implication, then, is that God chose some and not others of the nations and this is the same principle taught in the Reformed view of election—that God has the right to choose some and not others.

The Apostle Paul states in Ephesians 1:5, "He predestined us to adoption as sons through Jesus Christ to himself, according to the kind intention of His will." F. F. Bruce states that the ground of God's choosing must be sought exclusively in his own gracious

---

[12] Bruce Ware, "Divine Election to Salvation: Unconditional, Individual, and Infralapsarian," in *Perspectives on Election: 5 Views*, ed. Chad Owen Brand (Nashville: Broadman and Holman, 2006), 2. Ware writes, "Unconditional election refers to the claim that God's selection of those whom He would save was not based upon (or, not 'conditioned' on) some fact or feature of those individuals' lives, in particular. That is, God's election of those who would be saved was not conditioned on something they would do, some choice they would make, how good or bad they might be, or anything else specifically true about them in contrast to others also enslaved to sin deserving God's just condemnation."

character.[13] This reality is echoed in 2 Timothy 1:9 when the apostle states, "Who saved us and called us with a holy calling, not according to our works, but according to His own purpose and grace which was granted us in Christ Jesus from all eternity." The emphasis of the Reformed doctrine of election is that God elected His people out of His great love and freely chose to extend mercy to them out of nothing less than a pure act of grace.

The Scriptures teach that there is nothing meritorious in man whereby salvation would be granted based on a condition that was fulfilled. The Apostle Paul in Romans 9, when speaking of Jacob and Esau, states, "For though the twins were not yet born and had not done anything good or bad, so that God's purpose according to His choice would stand, not because of works but of him who calls." Commenting on Romans 9:10-13, Hendriksen states: "What Paul is saying, then, is this: In the final analysis the reason why some people are accepted and others rejected is because God so willed it. Human responsibility is not canceled, but there is no such thing as human merit. God's eternal purpose is not ultimately based on human works."[14] In other words, God's choice of Jacob over Esau was not because of anything that he foresaw in either whether good or bad, but solely according to His right to do as he pleases. For those chosen of God, there are no qualities, actions, or choices whereby the Holy One would be obligated or persuaded to grant His salvation to sinful, unregenerate rebels. He does so by a pure act of grace. God has ultimate freewill to do whatever he pleases in heaven on the earth (Ps 135:6). While there are certain areas of this view of election that

---

[13] F. F. Bruce, *The Epistle to the Ephesians: A Verse by Verse Exposition* (Calverton Down, UK: Creative Communications Ltd, 2012), 21. He writes, "The ground of God's choice, of his foreordaining us to be his sons, cannot be found in us. It was not because he foresaw something acceptable in us, not even because he foreknew that we would believe the gospel, that he singled us out for such an honor as this. The ground must be sought exclusively in his own gracious character; being the God he is, he willed and decreed our adoption as his sons, our conformity to his image, and in the fullness of time he sent his Son through whom alone this loving purpose could be made effective."

[14] Hendriksen, *Romans*, NTC (Grand Rapids: Baker Academic, 2007), 320.

are agreed upon by Arminian Christians, there are striking differences also.

Corporate Election

One of the differing views of election is the corporate view. This view teaches that "the elect" is the "Elect One" who is Christ, and individual election is recognized only in Christ; meaning, that God does not choose individuals unto salvation, but rather chose Christ. All who believe in Christ are elect because they are incorporated into Christ, the Elect One. Robert Shank, a proponent of this view, states, "the first step toward a correct understanding of the biblical doctrine of election is the recognition that the election of men is comprehended only in Christ; outside of Christ there is no election of any man."[15] With reference to Christ Jesus being elect of the Father, the Father says of the Son, "Behold, My Servant whom I have chosen; My Beloved in whom My soul is well-pleased" (Matt 12:18), and "This is My Son, My chosen One; listen to him" (Luke 9:35). This view of election, then, is not to be understood as the election of individuals, but of Christ only.

Roger Olson agrees that the Scriptures teach a corporate view of election. Olson agreeably quotes Arminian theologian William Klein who gives a thorough understanding of this position:

> When it comes to the provision of salvation and the determination of its benefits and blessings, the language of the New Testament writers is commanding. God decreed in his sovereign will to provide for salvation, and then he set Jesus on a course to secure it through his human life, death, and resurrection (Heb 10:9–10). He purposed to extend mercy to his people and to harden and punish unbelievers. He predestined or predetermined what believers will enjoy by virtue of

---

[15] Robert Shank, *Elect in the Son: A Study of the Doctrine of Election* (Minneapolis: Bethany House Publishers, 1989), 27.

their position in Christ. We may trace salvation and all that it entails solely to the pleasurable will of God.[16]

In other words, God's will does not determine the specific individuals who will receive that salvation, but determines what those individuals who come to Christ will enjoy in him. The language of "willing" embraces all, not a select number. God's will is not restrictive; he wills all to be saved. Yet, people can procure salvation only on God's terms.

According to the proponents of this view, though Jesus desires to reveal God to all, only those who come to him in faith find God and the salvation he offers. That some fail to find salvation can be attributed only to their unwillingness to believe—to their preference for their own way rather than God's. If God desires salvation for all, he wills (in a stronger sense) to give life to those who believe. For the advocates of the corporate view, these ideas are not incompatible. They place the initiative with God for providing salvation and the obligation with people to receive it on God's terms—faith in Christ. God has done more than merely provide salvation; he "draws" people (John 6:44) so they come to Christ. In fact, people come to Christ because God enables them (John 6:65). However, these actions of drawing and enablement are neither selective (only some are chosen for it), nor are they irresistible. Jesus's crucifixion was God's means of drawing all people to Christ (John 12:32). It was God's provision for their salvation. All may respond to God's overture, but they must do so by placing their trust in Christ. Since God draws all via the cross, and he desires that all repent of their sins and find salvation, it is not God's will that determines precisely which individuals will find salvation. Though God surely has always known who they will be, and though he gathers them as a body in Christ, individuals must repent and believe for God's will to be done.[17]

---

[16] Olsen, *Against Calvinism*, 130.

[17] William Klein, *The New Chosen People: A Corporate View of Election* (Eugene, OR: Wipf & Stock, 2015), 261.

Within these statements from William Klein one identifies several ingredients that characterize the corporate view: God predetermined not individuals unto salvation but the Lord Jesus and the benefits those in Christ receive; the atonement is for all; God desires the salvation of all; God draws all men; God enables all to respond to the gospel; those who believe are free to choose Christ and thereby become the elect of God; and, interestingly, an admission that God has always known who would believe. Robert Shank states that every man is elect in Jesus unless he chooses to remove himself and isolate himself from God.[18] In summary with reference to election and salvation, God chooses no one individually unto salvation but chose all and chose Christ to be the means that salvation would be accomplished and predetermined that all who freely call upon the Lord Jesus are elect in him and God has predetermined certain benefits for them.

Vocational Election

The corporate view of election also incorporates a doctrine of individual election. William Klein writes that when the Scriptures reference the election of individuals, it is in reference to God's choice of them for service. He goes on to say, "God has often chosen specific individuals to serve his purposes in the world, and this choice is a matter separate from their eternal salvation."[19] Klein writes of kings, priests, prophets, Pharaoh, and emperors that God called and used to accomplish his purposes. Roger Olsen agrees that this is an alternative to Calvinistic election, as does James Daane, saying, "Election in biblical thought is never a selection, a taking of this and a rejection of that out of multiple realities. Rather election is a call to service, a summons to be a co-laborer with God in the actualization of God's elective purpose and goal."[20] In other words, God's election of particular

---

[18] Robert Shank, *Elect in the Son*, 106.

[19] William Klein, *The New Chosen People: A Corporate View of Election* (Eugene, OR: Stock Publishers, 2015), 139.

[20] Cited in Olsen, *Against Calvinism*, 125.

individuals in the Scripture had nothing to do with salvation but of selecting them to serve him in a certain capacity. For example, author Shawn Lazar states that "God knew Jeremiah, and set him apart and appointed him to be a prophet [Jer 1:5]. And why did God know or choose Jeremiah? For eternal life? No. As the text says, he was chosen before conception to serve as a prophet to Israel. Jeremiah's election was vocational."[21] Lazar also speaks of Moses's election to service as evidence for his position that God elects individuals to service and not salvation.[22]

Cottrell, though not an adherent to the corporate election view, also sees an election to service in Romans 9 with some variation. Cottrell speaks of the two "Israels" in Romans 9 being two distinct groups: ethnic Israel and spiritual Israel. He identifies ethnic Israel as chosen by God, not for salvation, but for service, while identifying the spiritual Israel as those receiving salvation. He states, "The only approach to Romans 9 that truly addresses the issue of God's righteousness as it relates to ethnic Israel is that the election spoken of in verses 7–18 is election to service."[23] Cottrell adds that ethnic Israel's election was utilitarian, not redemptive, as God chose them for a purpose.[24] As a result of Cot-

---

[21] Shawn Lazar, *Chosen to Service: Why Divine Election is to Service, Not to Eternal Life* (Denton, TX: Grace Evangelical Society, 2017), 35.

[22] Lazar, *Chosen to Service*, 33. He writes, "We're all familiar with Moses's story. As the Bible tells us, Moses was born a Hebrew, raised as a prince of Egypt, fled to the wilderness, returned to Egypt as an old man, demanded that Pharaoh let his people go, and then led the Hebrews out of Egypt, across the Red Sea. Suffice it to say, Moses understood that he was chosen by God. But why? For eternal life? No. To accomplish an important mission: Moses said, 'By this you shall know that the LORD has sent me to so all these deeds; for this is not my doing.'"

[23] Jack Cottrell, "The Classical Arminian View of Election," in *Perspectives on Election: 5 Views*, ed. Chad Owen Brand (Nashville, Broadman and Holman, 2006), 124.

[24] Cottrell, "Classical Arminian View," 125. "God's covenant promises to physical Israel as such had to do only with the role of the nation in God's historical plan of redemption. Their election was utilitarian, not redemptive. God chose them to serve a purpose. The Jews themselves thought that this election

trell's view of Romans 9, he maintains that the Calvinist or Reformed view of Romans 9 is mistaken to interpret the chapter as dealing with election to salvation.

Individual Election

Cottrell has similar views to that of Klein, Shanks, and Lazar, but differs with them on his overall view of the doctrine of election. Cottrell is a classical Arminian and sees salvation as individual, but grounded in God's foreknowledge. He writes, "It [the classical Arminian doctrine of predestination] is the view that before the world ever existed God conditionally predestined some specific individuals to eternal life and the rest to eternal condemnation, based on his foreknowledge of their freewill responses to his law and to his grace."[25] He goes on to state that the key idea of classical Arminianism is the idea that God predestines according to foreknowledge (prescience) of future human freewill decisions. It is important to note that Cottrell defines the Greek word, *proorizo̅*, as meaning "to determine beforehand, to predetermine, to foreordain," and goes on to state that "predestination is thus God's predetermination or decision to do something, to cause something, to bring about a certain event or state of affairs at a future time."[26] In this Arminian view of predestination, God predetermines beforehand (prior to the creation of all things) that he will do something, or rather, he foreordains something to occur, based on His foreknowledge of the future events and people.

Though Cottrell sees the act of God's election as an election to service in certain passages of Scripture, he nevertheless rejects the corporate view of election and takes the view of election as individual election unto salvation. He writes, "Without question, when the Bible speaks of predestination to salvation, it refers to

---

involved the promise of salvation for individuals, but they were simply mistaken."

[25] Cottrell, "Classical Arminian View," 72.

[26] Cottrell, "Classical Arminian View," 74.

persons and not to an impersonal plan," and adds, "One cannot believe in predestination according to foreknowledge and at the same time deny individual predestination."[27] Cottrell acknowledges that some passages may refer to a corporate body that is called "the elect" but adds that the reality of the group, the corporate elect, presupposes individual election.

Thus far, Cottrell has put forth a view that is similar to my own in the sense of God predestinating individuals, but it will be in this next area where the differences emerge quite clearly. Cottrell states that God predetermines the end of salvation, but not the means of salvation. He argues that God "predetermines to give salvation to all believers, but he does not predestine certain unbelievers to become believers and the rest to remain in their unbelief."[28] He goes on to say that those who accept Christ through faith do so of their own free choice and that their choice of Jesus Christ is not predestined, but is foreknown. Once they choose Christ, they become the chosen ones.[29]

This view is not too dissimilar from that espoused by the Arminian theologian Norman Geisler. Geisler states, "As far as the Bible is concerned, there is no contradiction between divine predestination and human free choice."[30] Geisler maintains the same position as that of Cottrell that men can freely choose or not choose to come to Christ, and the choice that is made by them is not determined by God, but is of their own accord. Geisler, as stated in the previous section, states his logic in this manner:

> God knows all things. Whatever God foreknows must come to pass (i.e., is predetermined). God foreknew the Apostle John would accept Christ. Therefore, it had to come to pass

---

[27] Cottrell, "Classical Arminian View," 80.

[28] Cottrell, "Classical Arminian View," 81.

[29] Cottrell, "Classical Arminian View," 81. Cottrell writes, "Those who accept Christ through faith do so of their own free choice. Their choice of Jesus Christ is not predestined. That choice, however, is foreknown; and as a result, the choosing ones become the chosen ones, who are then predestined to receive the full blessings of salvation. Scripture itself says nothing about individuals being predestined to believe."

[30] Geisler, *Chosen but Free*, 38.

(as predetermined) that John would accept Christ. But here again John's acceptance is free. It is simply that God knowingly predetermined from all eternity that John would freely accept Christ.[31]

In addressing this mystery between God's foreknowledge and freewill, Geisler states:

How can one and same event be both free and determined at the same time? The answer, as the early St. Augustine put it, is that our free actions are determined from the standpoint of God's foreknowledge, but they are free from the vantage point of our choice. He noted that "no one sins because God foreknew that he would sin." So, "No man sins unless it is his choice to sin; and his choice not to sin, that, too, God foresaw. What St. Thomas Aquinas added—"Everything known by God must necessarily be"—is true if it refers to the statement of truth of God's knowledge, but it is false if it refers to the necessity of the contingent events. That is, our acts are free with respect to our choice, but they are determined with respect to God's foreknowledge of them.[32]

In stating this more clearly, Geisler says that God is omniscient, and as a result, eternally foreknew who would be saved. And "since His foreknowledge is infallible, whatever God foreknows will indeed come to pass." He adds, "Hence, His foreknowledge of who would be saved assures that they will be."[33] Geisler lists Romans 8:29 ("Those whom he foreknew") and 1 Peter 1:2 ("According to the foreknowledge of God") as evidence for his position, for both refer to God's foreknowledge.

In summing up this view of individual election, it is important to note that the corporate view and the conditional individual election view do not teach that man is able to come to

---

[31] Geisler, *Chosen but Free*, 43.

[32] Geisler, *Chosen but Free*, 45.

[33] Norman Geisler, *Systematic Theology in One Volume* (Bloomington, MI: Bethany House Publishers, 2011), 843.

Christ left to themselves. They both affirm the need for God's grace, but interpret God's grace not in the sense of God bringing about the necessary heart change, but simply as an enlightenment of understanding given to all. For example, Geisler puts forth the view held commonly by Arminians and non-Calvinists, which is called "prevenient grace" as discussed previously. Geisler writes, "Prevenient means 'before' and prevenient grace refers to God's unmerited work in the human heart prior to salvation, which directs people to this end through Christ."[34] Olsen agrees and states that prevenient grace is "the illuminating, convicting, calling, and enabling power of the Holy Spirit working on the sinner's soul and making them free to choose saving grace (or reject it)."[35] In other words, those who espouse prevenient grace assume that the person in their natural state is in darkness, and the Lord enables them to understand the gospel; it is at this point the person can either accept or reject the free offer of the gospel of Christ. Cottrell holds a somewhat different view of prevenient grace and states that it does not matter which view of prevenient grace one holds–whether it is given at birth until the age of accountability or in a later time through the Holy Spirit's intervention. What matters in his view is that when the gospel is proclaimed to the sinner, he is not in a state of total inability. He can respond by his own volition without the selective, irresistible act of the Holy Spirit because of the gift of prevenient grace to all mankind without distinction.[36]

The charge against the unconditional individual election adherents, like myself, is that we do not allow freewill but instead embrace divine determinism because of the denial of libertarian freewill. But this doctrine of prevenient grace renders libertarian freewill supposedly to the creature as Arminians believe God intended. How this prevenient grace operates can be illustrated as follows:

---

[34] Geisler, *Systematic Theology in One Volume*, 843.

[35] Olsen, *Against Calvinism*, 67.

[36] Cottrell, "Classical Arminian View," 121.

The classical Arminian believes that God steals into the prison and makes it to the bedside of the victim. God injects a serum that begins to clear the prisoner's mind of delusions and quell her hostile reactions. God removes the gag from the prisoner's mouth and shines a flashlight around the pitch-black room. The prisoner remains mute as the Rescuer's voice whispers, "Do you know where you are? Let me tell you! Do you know who you are? Let me show you!" And as the wooing begins, divine truth begins to dawn on the prisoner's heart and mind; the Savior holds up a small mirror to show the prisoner her sunken eyes and frail body. "Do you see what they've done to you, and do you see how you've given yourself to them?" Even in the dim light, the prisoner's weakened eyes are beginning to focus. The Rescuer continues, "Do you know who I am, and that I want you for myself?" Perhaps the prisoner makes no obvious advance but does not turn away. The questions keep coming: "Can I show you a picture of who you once were and the wondrous plans I have or you in the years to come?" The prisoner's heartbeat quickens as the Savior presses on: "I know that part of you suspects that I have come to harm you. But let me show you something—my hands, they're a bit bloody. I crawled through an awful tangle of barbed wire to get to you." Now here in this newly created sacred space, in this moment of new possibility, the Savior whispers, "I want to carry you out of here right now! Give me your heart! Trust me!" This scenario, we believe, captures the richness of the Bible's message.[37]

The doctrine of prevenient grace allows sinners to regain their freewill, while presenting the calling of God to them as a wooing or a compelling, but not a calling that is irresistible in changing the disposition of the soul through the regenerating work of the Spirit.

In the Arminian views that have been discussed, there are a few differences between them concerning the corporate election

---

[37] Jerry L. Walls and Joseph R. Dongell, *Why I Am Not a Calvinist* (Downers Grove: IVP, 2004), 69.

vs. individual election, but both views agree that God does not predestine anyone unconditionally unto salvation. For the individual election view, the main thrust of the argument is that election is based on God's foreknowledge of what people will do. In that sense, salvation is conditioned on faith, which is indeed acknowledged by Cottrell, Geisler, and Olsen. God foresaw those who would believe, and therefore, all whom he foresaw will come to Christ through the gospel. This, once again, places man in the place of authority in the realm of his salvation. It was contingent upon him believing, and God honors the exercising of his faith to elect him. What does this produce in the believer? Does it produce a genuine, deep appreciation for God's grace? No, because this kind of view diminishes God's grace, His sovereign work in regeneration, and elevates man more so than our Lord. Would this view of God's working in salvation result in greater praise to him? No, because man may take a degree of credit for his own salvation. Here again, the life of the believer is affected by his view of God's sovereignty in salvation. It has also been stated that God does not predestine anyone to believe, but rather predestines the result of those who believe that they will have eternal life with the Lord, and this view only attempts to bypass the reality of God's sovereign grace in the salvation of sinners . Since we have an understanding of these different views, we will look at some of the opposing arguments in the next chapter.

Questions for Reflection

1. What are the differences you see between election and reprobation?
2. Has God determined the destinies of all people? Why or why not?
3. Do you agree that election and reprobation are not symmetrical?
4. Is man deserving of God's election unto salvation?
5. Do you view the doctrine of election as being corporate or individual?

Chapter Four
Foreseen Faith or Foreordained Faith?

"For Scripture everywhere proclaims that God finds nothing in man to induce him to show kindness, but that he prevents him by free liberality. What can a dead man do to obtain life? But when he enlightens us with the knowledge of himself, he is said to raise us from the dead, and make us new creatures."[1]

Before heading into the last section of this book, inevitably, there will be questions about certain passages of Scripture that seem to teach God's universal love and desire for all to come to salvation. These are the "What about this Scripture?" passages that are often brought up against Reformed theologians by the Arminian camp as a rebuttal to the Reformed position. It is necessary to discuss these texts so as to leave no stone unturned. The focus of the book is the relationship between election and sanctification, therefore, these passages need to be explained in light of their context to demonstrate that they are not contrary to Reformed theology, and therefore not opposed to unconditional, individual election.

The first passage we will look at will help us to establish that faith is a gift of God and does not originate within ourselves. In having this correct understanding, it will be apparent that God does not foresee faith in any as assumed by the Arminian camp because none have faith in and of themselves apart from God. The next passage will expound the true meaning of the word,

---

[1] John Calvin, *Institutes of the Christian Religion* (Peabody, MA: Hendriksen Publishers, 2008), 505.

"foreknew," in order that we can know what it actually means in contrast to how it is used today by Arminians.

As we head into the Scripture to look at these specific passages, it should be noted that there are some truths that we all share within the differing views of election that have been discussed and expounded briefly.

The Agreeables

There are indeed elements of all these views that are true and grounded within Scripture. The Scriptures do teach an election unto service. MacArthur and Mayhue state, "Scripture employs the terminology of election in several senses."[2] First, Scripture teaches that God elects certain individuals unto service. MacArthur and Mayhue write:

> God is said to choose, or elect, certain people either to an office or to perform a specific task of service. He chose people for leadership over the nation of Israel, as in the case of Moses (Num 16:5-7) and Zerubbabel (Hag 2:23). Scripture indicates that God chose those whom he pleased to the priestly ministry of Israel, both the tribe of Levi in general (Deut 18:1-5; 21:5; 1 Chron 15:2) and men individually (e.g., 1 Sam 2:27-28). As with the office of priest, so also God elected his chosen ones to serve in the offices of king (Deut 17:15; 1 Sam 10:24; 1 Chron 28:4-6; 29:1) and prophet (Jer 1:10).[3]

MacArthur and Mayhue list numerous places in Scripture where God chose whomever he desired to do something in service to him. This is a truth that is grounded in Scripture, and it is here that the Reformed theologian, the corporate election adherent, and the Arminian agree.

---

[2] MacArthur and Mayhue, *Biblical Doctrine*, 494.

[3] MacArthur and Mayhue, *Biblical Doctrine*, 494.

The teaching of corporate election is also taught in Scripture. This view, as discussed earlier, understands election as an election of a body or group of people. It is not as Karl Barth maintained with the whole of the human race being chosen by God, but rather a group of people or a nation being selected by God out of all humanity. It is also not in the manner of that of William Klein and Robert Shank, which claims a hypothetical group of people elect in Christ, the Elect One. The primary example of this category of election is the election of Israel by the Lord. Israel, as Louis Berkhof states, was elected by the Lord for special purposes and privileges.[4] MacArthur and Mayhue agree and write that Israel was chosen to be the recipients of God's covenant love and blessings.[5] This view of corporate election indeed differs from what was discussed earlier, but there is certainly a category of corporate election taught in the Bible in the manner just discussed.

The third view of election is certainly found within God's Word. It is here that the Reformed theologian and Arminian theologian agree, but only up to a point. Certainly, God has chosen individuals unto salvation; however, the point of separation is whether or not God's election was conditional or unconditional. The Reformed perspective sees no proof of "prevenient grace" in Scripture as discussed previously. Mankind does not have the faith or the ability to come to Christ unless there is a fundamental change in the disposition of the soul. Wihelmus á Brakel states, "Man is totally blind as far as spiritual things are concerned," and, " by nature is of such a wicked and evil disposition that he is not willing to repent, nor can he will to do so, for he cannot

---

[4] Berkhof, *Systematic Theology*, 114.

[5] MacArthur and Mayhue, *Biblical Doctrine*, 495. They write, "As Moses declared the law of God to the second generation of Israelites preparing to enter the Promised Land, he insisted that their covenant relationship with Yahweh was rooted in his sovereign election."

respond with his will to that which he does not know."[6] The emphasis here is that man cannot exercise a faith in Christ that he does not possess, and this emphasis is in opposition to the Arminian view that God foresaw a people exercising faith in Christ, and thus meeting the condition for salvation. Steven Lawson states, "No corpse can raise itself from the grave. Neither can any spiritually dead sinner believe upon Christ. God must act sovereignly to make the sinner spiritually alive before he can exercise saving faith."[7] Lawson adds, "Saving faith is a gift that God must give."[8]

A Faith from God

The foundation of the view that faith is a gift of God and does not originate with man is grounded in Ephesians 2:8–9: "For by grace you have been saved through faith; and that not of yourselves, it is the gift of God; not as a result of works, so that no one may boast." Geisler states:

However plausible this interpretation ['that' referring to 'faith'] may seem in English, it is very clear from the Greek that Ephesians 2:8–9 is not referring to faith as a gift from God. For the 'that" (*touto*) is neuter in the form and cannot

---

[6] Wilhelmus á Brakel, *The Christian's Reasonable Service: The Church and Salvation*, vol. 2 (Grand Rapids: Reformation Heritage Books, 2015), 216–17. He writes, "Man is totally blind as far as spiritual things are concerned. 'Having the understanding darkened, being alienated from the life of God through the ignorance that is in them' (Eph. 4:18); 'But as it is written, Eye hath not seen. . . . But the natural man receiveth not the things of the Spirit of God: for they are foolishness unto him: neither can he know them, because they are spiritually discerned' (1 Cor 2:9, 14). . . . Someone who is blind to such a degree can neither will, repent of himself, nor believe in Christ, even if he hears the Gospel."

[7] Steven Lawson, *Foundations of Grace: 1400BC–AD100*, vol. 1 (Sanford, FL: Reformation Trust Publishing), 423.

[8] Lawson, *Foundations of Grace*, 423.

refer to 'faith' (*pistis*), which is feminine. The antecedent of 'it is the gift of God' is the salvation by grace through faith.[9]

Geisler appeals to A. T. Robertson as an authority for his position.[10] William Hendriksen, commenting on the same statement from Robertson concerning the Greek grammar in Ephesians 2:8–9, writes:

> Commenting on this passage, in his [A.T. Robertson's] *Word Pictures in the New Testament*, he states, "grace is God's part, faith ours." He adds that since in the original the demonstrative "this" (and this not of yourselves) is neuter and does not correspond with the gender of the word "faith," which is feminine, it does not refer to the latter "but to the act of being saved by grace conditioned on faith on our part." Without any hesitancy I answer, Robertson, to whom the entire world of New Testament scholarship is heavily indebted, does not express himself felicitously in this instance. This is true first because in a context in which the apostle places such a tremendous stress on the fact that from start to finish man owes his salvation to God, to him alone, it would have been very strange, indeed, for him to say, "Grace is God's part, faith is ours." True though it be that both the responsibility of believing and also its activity are ours, for God does not believe for us, nevertheless, in the present context one rather expects emphasis on the fact that both in its initiation and its continuation faith is entirely dependent on God, and so is our complete salvation. Also, Robertson, a grammarian famous in his field, knew that in the original the demonstrative (this, though neuter, by no means always corresponds in gender with its antecedent. That he knew this is shown by the fact that on the indicated page of his Grammar (p. 704) he points

---

[9] Geisler, *Chosen but Free*, 189.

[10] A. T. Robertson, *Word Pictures in the New Testament* (Nashville: Broadman Press, 1931), 4:525. Robertson writes, "'Grace' is God's part, 'faith' ours. And that [it] (*kai touto*) is neuter, not feminine *taute*, and so refers not to *pistis* [faith] or to *charis* [grace] (feminine also), but to the act of being saved by grace conditioned on faith on our part."

out that "in general" the demonstrative "agrees with its substantive in gender and number." When he says "in general," he must mean, "not always but most of the time." Hence, he should have considered more seriously the possibility that, in view of the context, the exception to the rule, an exception by no means rare, applies here. He should have made allowance for it. Finally, he should have justified the departure from the rule that unless there is a compelling reason to do otherwise the antecedent should be looked for in the immediate vicinity of the pronoun or adjective that refers to it.[11]

Hendriksen points out that Geisler and Robertson both appeal to this same rule in Greek Grammar. However, Robertson does not allow for the exception to the rule whose existence he acknowledged in his other writings. Lawson and Hendriksen adhere to the view that the closest antecedent to "that" is "faith," and its meaning is that faith is a gift of God and does not originate within man. Though agreeable to the truth that faith is a gift of God, Daniel Wallace also includes grace and salvation as a whole as the gift of God in Ephesians 2:8. He writes, "While it is true that on rare occasions there is a gender shift between antecedent and pronoun, the pronoun is almost always caught between two nouns of different gender. One is the antecedent; the other is the predicate nominative."[12] He states:

This is the most debated text in terms of the antecedent of the demonstrative pronoun, *touto*. The standard interpretations include: (1) "grace" as antecedent, (2) "-faith" as antecedent, (3) the concept of a grace–by–faith salvation as antecedent, and (4) *kai touto* having an adverbial force with no anteced-

[11] William Hendriksen, *Galatians, Ephesians, Philippians, Colossians, and Philemon*, NTC (Grand Rapids: Baker Academic, 2007), 121.

[12] Daniel B. Wallace, *Greek Grammar: Beyond the Basics* (Grand Rapids: Zondervan, 1996), 334.

ent ("and especially"). The issues here are complex and cannot be solved by grammar alone. Nevertheless, syntactical considerations do tend toward one of the latter two views.[13]

Wallace adds, "More plausible is the third view that *touto* refers to the concept of a grace-by-faith salvation. As we have seen, *touto* regularly takes a conceptual antecedent."[14] Though there are differing views when identifying the antecedent, the overall truth is not changed. Whether faith alone is the antecedent, or the entirety of salvation which includes faith is the antecedent, faith still remains a gift of God. The implication, then, is that there could not have been any foreseen faith by God, for none have any faith unless it is granted to him by the Lord, and this is the view of the Reformed camp.

Those He Foresaw (Romans 8:29)

A crucial passage in the debate of doctrine of election argument is Romans 8:29. This passage contains the phrase, "Those whom he foreknew." This passage would seem to imply the Arminian view that God simply knew the future or future decisions by sinners. In actuality, though, this word does not mean, "foresaw." The Greek word "foreknew" is *proegno* of the root *proginosko*, which means, "to foreknow, to appoint as the subject of future privileges."[15] Arminians, as discussed earlier, take a position similar to that of Frank Page who stated, "God knew who was going to be saved and as a part of that foreknowledge he guarantees that those who have accepted Christ will become like His Son, Jesus Christ."[16] As stated earlier, Cottrell and Geisler

---

[13] Daniel B. Wallace, *The Basics of New Testament Syntax: An Intermediate Greek Grammar* (Grand Rapids: Zondervan, 2000), 183.

[14] Wallace, *Greek Grammar*, 334.

[15] Mounce, *Analytical Lexicon to the Greek New Testament*, 390.

[16] Frank Page, *Trouble with the TULIP* (Canton, GA: Riverstone Group Publishing, 2006), 70.

quote Romans 8:29 as a proof text against the Reformed view of election. Sproul, however, states the following:

> Perhaps the greatest weakness of the foreknowledge view is the text cited as its greatest strength. On a closer analysis, the passage in Romans cited above (Romans 8:29) becomes a serious problem for the foreknowledge view. On the one hand those who appeal to it to support the foreknowledge view find too little. That is, the passage teaches less than the advocates of foreknowledge would like it teach and yet teaches more than they want it to teach. How can this be? First, the conclusion that God's predestination is determined by God's foreknowledge is not taught in the passage. Paul does not come out and say that God chooses people on the basis of his prior knowledge of their choices. That idea is neither stated nor implied by the text. All the text declares is that God predestines those whom he foreknows. No one in this debate disputes that God has foreknowledge. Even God could not choose people he didn't know anything about. Before he could choose Jacob he had to have some idea in his mind of Jacob. But the text does not teach that God chose Jacob on the basis of Jacob's choice.[17]

Sproul's point is that the Arminian camp appeals to this verse as a proof-text that salvation is based on God's foreknowledge of what he knew people would do. However, the passage never states this idea.

This passage becomes even more troublesome for the foreknowledge advocates when Romans 8:30 is examined in light of verse 29. Sproul brings attention to the order of events throughout verses 29 and 30: foreknowledge, predestination, calling, justification, and glorification. The problem for the Arminians, he states, is the relationship between "calling" and "justification."[18] Sproul points out that the implication of the text is that all whom God calls, he justifies. This is in direct opposition to the

---

[17] Sproul, *Chosen by God*, 105.

[18] Sproul, *Chosen by God*, 105.

Arminian view that God calls all people. MacArthur and Mayhue write:

> It is to be observed that the calling Paul has in view here is the effectual call of God that results in salvation, rather than a general calling that may be rejected. This is so because he says that all those who are thus called are also justified and glorified. No one who hears this calling fails to receive the saving blessings of justification and glorification.[19]

The implication of this text as pointed out by Sproul and MacArthur is that this passage does not state that God foresaw faith in anyone, and very directly concludes that all whom God calls are those he justifies. It is not said that all whom God saw exercising faith were called, or all people everywhere are called. As stated earlier, "foreknew" means, "to appoint as the subject of future privileges, to determine on beforehand, to be previously acquainted with."[20] God knew intimately those whom he would choose and "determined beforehand" these whom he would call. Sproul states, "If all whom God calls inwardly are justified and all whom God predestines are called inwardly, then it follows that God's foreknowledge concerns more than a mere prior awareness of the free decisions humans will make."[21] In opposition to this interpretation, Geisler states, "There is strong evidence to show that 'foreknow' does not mean 'choose' or 'elect' in the Bible. For one thing, many verses use the same root word for knowledge of persons where there is no personal relationship."[22] Geisler goes on to state that the extreme Calvinist's equation of foreknowing and foreloving does not follow.[23]

---

[19] MacArthur and Mayhue, *Biblical Doctrine*, 568.

[20] Mounce, *Analytical Lexicon to the Greek New Testament*, 390.

[21] Sproul, *Chosen By God*, 108. Sproul goes on to state, "God does know from all eternity who will respond to the gospel and who will not. But such knowledge is not that of a mere passive observer. God knows from eternity whom he will inwardly call. All whom he inwardly calls he will also justify."

[22] Geisler, *Chosen but Free*, 71.

[23] Geisler, *Chosen but Free*, 71.

Hendriksen, however, takes an opposing view to that of Geisler, arguing that foreknowledge means divine active delight.[24] Hendriksen states, "It [God's divine active delight] indicates that, in his own sovereign good pleasure, God set his love on certain individuals, many still to be born, gladly acknowledging them as his own, electing them to everlasting life and glory."[25] Hendriksen then lists various Scriptures of God's intimate love for those he knew beforehand: "For I have known him [Abraham] so that he may direct his children and his household after him" (Gen 18:19); Before I formed you in the womb I knew you, before you were born I set you apart" (Jer 1:5); and lastly, "I am the Good Shepherd, and I know my own" (John 10:4). In addition to the above passages of Scripture, MacArthur and Mayhue write the following:

> The Greek verb *proginosko* in Romans 8:29 speaks not of simple foreknowledge but of the knowledge that characterizes an intimate personal relationship. There are two other places in the New Testament in which *proginosko* speaks of God's foreknowledge. In the first, the Apostle Peter writes, "He [Christ] was foreknown before the foundation of the world but was made manifest in the last times for the sake of you" (1 Pet 1:20). If foreknowledge means nothing than God looking ahead to see what is going to happen, this verse is meaningless. To be consistent with the simple-foreknowledge definition, one would have to say that this verse means that God looked down the corridors of time, discovered that Christ would willingly lay down his life for sinners, and then on that basis decided to appoint him the Mediator between God and man. Instead, Peter's intent is to point to the intimate knowledge of personal relationship between the Father and the Son in the Trinitarian counsel of redemption. The other occurrence comes in Romans 11:2, where Paul employs the term with respect to Israel, saying, "God has not rejected his people whom he foreknew." Once again, we cannot conclude

---

[24] Hendriksen, *Romans*, NTC, 282.

[25] Hendriksen, *Romans*, NTC, 282.

that Israel was the only people of whom God was aware; rather, Paul's point is to emphasize the intimate relationship between God and Israel founded on the covenants of promise.[26]

The passages quoted by MacArthur, Mayhue, and Hendriksen strongly argue that the word "foreknow" carries with it a much stronger meaning that simple knowledge of the future. In agreement with MacArthur and Mayhue, Thomas Schreiner writes that the background of the term "foreknow" should be understood in light of the use of the Old Testament Hebrew word, *yada*.[27] He writes,

> [Yada] refers to his [God's] covenant love, in which he sets his affection on those whom he has chosen. (Gen 18:19; Ex 33:17; 1 Sam 2:12; Ps 18:43; Prov 9:10; Jer 1:5; Hosea 13:5; Amos 3:2)...In Amos 3:2 God's knowledge of Israel, in contrast to that of the rest of the nations, can scarcely be cognitional only, since Yahweh had full knowledge of all nations of the earth. The intention of the text is to say that Yahweh had set his covenant love on only Israel. Romans 11:2 yields the same conclusion: "God has not rejected his people whom he foreknew." The verb *proegno* (foreknew) here functions as the antonym to *aposato* (rejected). In other words, the verse is saying that God has not rejected his people on whom he set his covenant love. Similarly, in Romans 8:29 the point is that God has predestined those on whom he has set his covenant affection. The object of the verb *proegno* (foreknew) is personal, "those whom" (*hous*) God has set his affection on. God foreknows not just facts about the world but specific persons. Nor is the focus here on God's foreknowledge of the church; instead, individual believers are in view.[28]

---

[26] MacArthur and Mayhue, *Biblical Doctrine*, 499.

[27] Schreiner, *Romans*, BECNT, 726.

[28] Schreiner, *Romans*, BECNT, 726–27.

The meaning of Romans 8:29, in keeping with the descriptions of God's relationship with his people, is that God sovereignly chose unconditionally to make His elect the objects of His gracious, covenant love.

Questions for Reflection

1. Do you understand the doctrine of election being unconditional individual election?
2. Is prevenient grace a biblical concept?
3. Is faith a gift, or is it already present in man?
4. Is faith foreseen or foreordained?
5. Do you see the certainty of all whom God calls receiving justification and glorification?

Chapter Five
The Savior of All

"Reason praises God when he saves the undeserving, but accuses him when he damns the undeserving."[1]

What about passages that refer to "all?" Does "all" always carry the meaning of the universality of mankind? In this chapter we will examine 2 Peter 3:9 and also 1 Timothy 2:4 and 1 Timothy 4:10. These Scriptures are interpreted by the Arminian camp to mean that God is the Savior of all men redemptively and desires to lose none. There are, of course, implications to having this view which affect one's view of God and of Christ and His work. We have to understand that when we believe something, we must follow out this belief to its logical conclusion. When we follow the Arminian view out, we see that God's sovereignty is reduced, once again, because God is wishing something that he is unable to bring to pass, and the work of Christ reduced to being for everyone in general and no one in particular. What happens then? Our growth in Christ is stalled because we have a diminished view of God, His grace, and His salvation in Christ. Let us then, examine these particular passages that we may understand them rightly, and know with certainty that they are not in opposition to the Reformed view.

Not Willing for Any to Perish (2 Peter 3:9)

In the writings of Norman Geisler, George Bryson, and the other Arminian theologians such as Roger Olsen, William Klein,

---

[1] Martin Luther, *Bondage of the Will* (Choteau, MT: Old Paths Gospel Press), 268.

and 2 Peter 3:9 is often quoted as a proof text against the Reformed position of predestination. The text of 2 Peter 3:9 states, "The Lord is not slow about His promise, as some count slowness, but is patient toward you, not wishing for any to perish but for all to come to repentance." Bryson states, "If Calvinism is right then this should read that God does not want any of the elect to perish."[2] Bryson is correct in his statement, though he makes it as a criticism. Geisler writes, "God is love, and as such '[he is] not willing that *any* should perish but that all should come to repentance' . . . and contrary to the unreasonable view of the extreme Calvinists, this does not mean 'all classes of men,' namely, the elect from all nations."[3]

Despite the criticisms from Bryson and Geisler, the interpretation of 2 Peter 3:9 that is most plausible with the context is that the apostle is speaking of believers when he says that God is not wishing for any to perish. The word *tinas* (any), which is a plural form of *tis*, has a variety of meanings in the Scripture. The same form in 2 Peter 3:9 is translated as "several" in Acts 9:19: "Now for *several* days he was with the disciples who were at Damascus." The root word *tis* is translated "some" in Hebrews 10:27. This is not to say that it always has a meaning of something being limited, but the point is that the word is determined by its context and does not always have a universal application. James Montgomery Boice and Philip Ryken state:

> 2 Peter 3:9 is not talking about the salvation of all men and women, but only of the elect. The issue is the delay of Christ's return, and Peter is explaining that God has delayed it, not out of indifference to us and what we may be suffering, but because he wants to bring to repentance all whom he has determined in advance will be gathered in. If Christ should come now, there would be generations of yet unborn people, containing generations of Christians yet to come, who would not be in heaven. Therefore, "The Lord is not slow in keeping

---

[2] George Bryson, *Five Points of Calvinism: Weighed and Found Wanting*, (Costa Mesa, CA: The Word for Today, 2006), 84.

[3] Geisler, *Chosen but Free*, 207.

his promise, as some understand slowness. He is patient with you, not wanting [any of his elect ones] to perish, but everyone to come to repentance."[4]

The object of the promise of God's will is the believers to whom Peter is writing. This is evident by the pronouns used throughout the epistle and the flow of thought in chapter 3.

The Apostle Peter speaks in chapters 2 and 3 of God punishing the wicked on the Day of Judgment. Peter says in 2:9 that the Lord is keeping the unrighteous under punishment for the Day of Judgment. He also states in 3:7 that "the present heavens and earth are being reserved for fire, kept for the Day of Judgment and destruction of ungodly men." God has made it clear that he will judge the wicked and ungodly. Throughout chapter 3:1-9 there are a number of uses of pronouns that involve the believers and unbelievers. In speaking of the "mockers" of the last days, Peter uses the words "their" and "they" to refer to them. These are the ungodly spoken of in verse 7 that are reserved for judgment. Peter also uses other pronouns to refer to believers: "Beloved," "you," and "your." MacArthur writes that the use of the pronoun "you" refers to Peter's immediate readers and not universally meaning everyone everywhere.[5] He goes on to state, "Some have argued that *you* implies the salvation of all people. But the immediate context and comments about 'the destruction of ungodly men' clearly limits the *you* to believers."[6]

Throughout Peter's second epistle, there are particular pronouns the apostle uses to refer to his audience whom he identifies as, "those who have received a faith of the same kind as ours." He uses first and second pronouns such as "us," "our," "we," "you," and "yours" to refer to the believers to whom his epistle is written (1:1). When 3:9 is examined, Peter states that

---

[4] James Montgomery Boice and Philip Graham Ryken, *The Doctrines of Grace: Rediscovering the Evangelical Gospel* (Wheaton: Crossway Books, 2002), 127.

[5] John MacArthur, *2 Peter and Jude*, MacNTC (Chicago: Moody Publishers, 2005), 122-23.

[6] MacArthur, *2 Peter and Jude*, MacNTC, 123.

the Lord is not slack concerning His promise but is patient toward "you" not willing for any to perish.

Lawson states that God is longsuffering toward sinners, providing time for the elect to be saved.[7] That is, God is not willing that "any of us" should perish, but that "all of us" come to repentance. This is in keeping with what Christ said; namely, that all that the Father has given to him will come. John Owen writes the following:

> Who are these of whom the apostle speaks, to whom he writes? Such as had received "great and precious promises," chap. 1:4, whom he calls "beloved" (chap. 3:1); whom he opposeth to the "scoffers" of the "last days," verse 3; to whom the Lord hath respect in the disposal of these days; who are said to be "elect" (Matt. 24:22). Now, truly, to argue that because God would have none of those to perish, but all of them to come to repentance, therefore, he hath the same will and mind towards all and everyone in the world (even those to whom he never makes known his will, nor ever calls to repentance, if they never once hear of his way of salvation), comes not much short of extreme madness and folly.[8]

The context of 2 Peter 3:9 supports the interpretation that Peter is referring to his audience who are believers, rather than to mankind universally.

The Savior of All Men (1 Timothy 2:4; 4:10)

These next two passages are a great cause of disagreement, and are often quoted to oppose the Reformed view of election. For example, George Bryson brings out a number of arguments against the Reformed doctrine of election, and states that if God has elected only some to salvation as Calvinism teaches, then

---

[7] Lawson, *Foundations of Grace*, 334.

[8] John Owen, "The Death of Death in the Death of Christ: A Treatise of the Redemption and Reconciliation That is in the Blood of Christ," *The Works of John Owen*, vol. 10, ed. William H. Goold (London: Banner of Truth, 1967), 173–74.

why did Paul state in 1 Timothy 2:4 that God desires "all men" to be saved and come to the knowledge of God?[9] Bryson is not alone in this interpretation of 1 Timothy 2:4. Walls and Dongell also state that this passage points towards God's universal saving intentions.[10] William Klein concludes that "Paul envisions God's 'will' to be variegated, so that what he wills (or genuinely wishes) is not what he always decrees or implements."[11] In other words, though God strongly desires something as important as the salvation of every single person, he does not interfere so as to accomplish what he desires.

The particular argument that the Lord desires all men to be saved rests on the word "all" in 1 Timothy 2:3, in verse 6, and in 1 Timothy 4:10, which states, "For it is for this we labor and strive, because we have fixed our hope on the living God, who is the Savior of all men, especially of believers." For the Arminian, the word "all" is universal in scope and cannot have any limitations to it. The question is, however, whether the Scripture uses the word "all" always in a universal sense. In Romans 5:18, the Apostle Paul states, "So then as through one transgression there resulted condemnation to all men, even so through one act of righteousness there resulted justification of life to all men." In this passage the apostle speaks of "all" being condemned universally, and uses the word "all" again in reference to those made righteous through Christ's obedience. It is clear that all men are sinners, but are all men made righteous in Christ? R. C. Sproul writes that every human being has been born with a sinful and corrupt nature as a result of the Fall of Adam and Eve.[12] This is

---

[9] George Bryson, *Five Points of Calvinism: Weighed and Found Wanting* (Costa Mesa, CA: The Word for Today, 2006), 83.

[10] Walls and Dongell, *Why I Am Not a Calvinist*, 51.

[11] William Klein, *New Chosen People*, 142. Klein goes on to state, "God's will is not always accomplished, because he does not always insist or determine that it is. It is God's strong desire, truly his will; it is the best outcome for people. The salvation of every single person is what God genuinely wants or desires, but he does not command or determine the outcome."

[12] Sproul, *Essential Truths of the Christian Faith*, 151. Sproul writes, "The Bi-

clear, for example, by the Apostle Paul in Romans 5:12: "Therefore, just as through one man sin entered into the world, and death through sin, and so death spread to all men, because all sinned." Though "all" are sinners through Adam, "all" are not saved in Christ according to a number of other passages, such as John 3:18 and Matthew 25:41, for example. The clear teaching of Scripture is that not all will be made righteous; therefore, the context of Romans 5:18 qualifies the word "all" to be universal in the first part and limited in the latter part. The use of the word "many" in Romans 5:19 ("many were made sinners . . . many will be made righteous) is synonymous with the use of "all" in verse 18, and both are qualified by the context.

Thomas Schreiner commenting on the apparent dilemma writes:

> Adam as the head of the human race sinned as our representative, and we are sinners by virtue of being in corporate solidarity with Adam. . . . As sons and daughters of Adam we enter the work spiritually dead and sinners. But God, in his grace, has reversed the baleful results of Adam's sin by imputing the righteousness of Christ to us . . . it is totally undeserved. . . . If all become sinners through the headship of Adam, then does it not follow that all shall be counted righteous through the headship of Christ? Paul seems to draw this very conclusion, since he specifically says that just as "many" (*polloi*) died (v. 15) and were counted sinners (v. 19) through the transgression of Adam, so too "many" (*polloi*) have received an abundance of grace and shall be counted righteous through the work of Christ. The universal character of Christ's work is strengthened by the thesis that *polloi* (many) is equivalent to *pantes* (all). The "many" who fell through Adam must refer to "all," and for the comparison to stand, the same must apply to the "many" who have received the grace of Christ. The equivalence between "many" (*polloi*) and "all"

---

ble clearly teaches that our original parents, Adam and Eve, fell into sin. Subsequently, every human being has been born with sinful and corrupt nature. If the Bible didn't explicitly teach this, we would have to deduce it rationally from the bare fact of the universality of sin."

(*pantes*) is substantiated by verse 18. There the condemnation brought by Adam impinges on "all people" (*pantes anthropous*), while the justification obtained by Christ also applies to "all people" (*pantes anthropous*). . . . As pictures or images of God's intentions, both statements have a message for human beings, but if we try to make both cohere propositionally, we must admit that Paul contradicts himself... The "many" (*polloi*) and "all" (*pantes*) who have been affected by Christ are not coterminous with the "many" (*polloi*) and "all" (*pantes*) affected by Adam's sin. The latter group is universal, but the former group is restricted to all those who belong to Christ. This is suggested as I have already argued, by the context of Romans as a whole. Chapters 1–4 stress that human beings must exercise faith to be justified, while chapters 5–8 insist that those who receive God's grace live a transformed life. . . . Universal language is used of Christ's work to signify that all people without distinction (both Jews and Gentiles) are the recipients of God's work, which is quite different from saying that all people without exception receive his grace.[13]

Schreiner goes on to state that "all" does not always mean every human being as is observed in the above explanation of Romans 5:18–19, and "here it [Romans 5:18] designates all those who belong to Christ."[14] If the word "all" in the second part of the verse is understood in a universal sense as in the first, then the implication is that all people everywhere will be justified. This, as Schreiner pointed out, is not consistent with the teaching of Scripture. Berkhof writes, "If the word 'all' is not interpreted in a limited sense, [it] would teach, not merely that Christ made salvation possible for all men, but that he actually saves all without exception."[15] Logically, unless one is a universalist, the word "all" is not speaking of everyone everywhere, but is limited in scope. This is also true in 1 Corinthians 15:22: "For as in Adam all die, so

---

[13] Schreiner, *Romans*, BECNT, 491–94.

[14] Schreiner, *Romans*, BECNT, 494.

[15] Berkhof, *Systematic Theology*, 396.

also in Christ Jesus all will be made alive."[16] When the context is examined, this limited implication of the word "all" is also applicable to the understanding of 1 Timothy 2:4-6 and 1 Timothy 4:10.

It is the contention of the Reformed view that the word translated "all" (*pantas*) in 1 Timothy 2:4 is not speaking in a universal sense of all people everywhere, but rather is speaking of "all" the types of men in existence. Paul begins chapter 2 by urging Timothy to pray on behalf of all men, for kings and all who are in authority. Having just told Timothy to pray for all men, Paul, then expounds on the kinds of men he is speaking about: kings and all who are in authority. As James White argued in his debate with Dave Hunt, what is in view in this passage is "kinds" of men.[17] It is not that Timothy should just pray for Christians or for the poor, or for the rich, or for only one particular people or class of people. He is to pray on behalf of all people, even kings and those who are in authority, meaning all kinds or all classes of people. This is echoed by John Calvin: "For the apostle simply means that there is no people and no rank in the world that is excluded from salvation; because God wishes that the gospel should be proclaimed to all without exception."[18] Therefore, when Paul states that God desires "all men" to be saved, he is meaning that God desires all kinds of men to be saved. The elect of God will come from all nations, tongues, and all classes of people.

The interpretation of 1 Timothy 4:10 is, however, a little more complex than 2:4-6. It states, "For it is for this we labor and strive, because we have fixed our hope on the living God, who is the Savior of all men, especially of believers." Whereas the Arminian adherents see this passage as proof of God's desire to save

---

[16] William Hendriksen states with regards to this passage, "Here is it clearly stated that the 'all' who will be made alive are those who are Christ's, that is those who belong to him . . . this answer proves that when Paul uses the expression 'all' or 'all men' in connection with those who are or will be saved, this 'all' or 'all men' must not be interpreted in the absolute or unlimited sense" (Hendriksen, *Romans*, NTC, 183).

[17] James White and Dave Hunt, *Debating Calvinism* (Colorado Springs, CO: Multnomah Books, 2004), 324.

[18] John Calvin, *I Timothy*, CC (Grand Rapids: Baker Books, 2009), 54-55.

all men, to the contrary, this passage does not state this. It is important to note that this passage does not say that God wants to save all men, but rather it states that he is the Savior of all men in some sense. The passage expresses the use of the word *sotēr* (savior, deliverer, preserver)[19] in a general sense as the LXX uses this word. William Hendriksen gives the example of Othniel who is referred to as a "deliverer" (*sotēr*) in Judges 3:9: "The Lord raised up a deliverer for the sons of Israel to deliver them, Othniel the son of Kenaz, Caleb's younger brother." Hendriksen writes that "in a sense all the judges of Israel were 'saviors' (deliverers), just as we read in Nehemiah 9:27."[20] Nehemiah 9:27 states, "Therefore You delivered them into the hand of their oppressors who oppressed them, but when they cried to You in the time of their distress, You heard from heaven, and according to Your great compassion You gave them deliverers (saviors) who delivered them from the hand of their oppressors."

This word *sotēr* is also used in a general sense of the Lord toward the people of Israel as Hendriksen points out.[21] Psalm 106:19-21 states: "They made a calf in Horeb and worshiped a molten image. Thus they exchanged their glory for the image of an ox that eats grass. They forgot God their Savior, who had done great things in Egypt." The psalmist here speaks of the first generation of Israelites who came out of Egypt, who tested the Lord, and ultimately was denied entrance into the Promised Land. Commenting on Psalm 106:21, MacArthur writes, "this title [God their Savior], common in the pastoral epistles, is seldom used in the Old Testament outside of Isaiah. Here, it refers to physical deliverance. It looks forward to Jesus Christ as spiritual redeemer."[22] Hendriksen writes:

---

[19] Mounce, *Analytical Lexicon to the Greek New Testament*, 442.

[20] William Hendriksen, *Thessalonians, the Pastorals, and Hebrews*, NTC (Grand Rapids: Baker Academic, 2007), 154.

[21] Hendriksen, *Thessalonians, the Pastorals, and Hebrews*, 154-55.

[22] John MacArthur, *The MacArthur Bible Commentary* (Nashville: Thomas Nelson, 2005), 670.

According to the Old Testament, then, God is *Sōtēr* not only of those who enter his everlasting kingdom but in a sense also of others, indeed, of all those whom he delivers from temporary disaster . . . God's kind providence extends to all men, in a sense even to plants and animals: Ps 36:6; 104:27; 145:9, 16, 17; Jonah 4:10, 11. He provides his creatures with food, keeps them alive, is deeply interested in them, often delivers them from disease, ills, hurt, famine, war, poverty, and peril in any form. He is, accordingly, their *Sōtēr* (Preserver, Deliverer, and in that sense Savior).

Hendriksen explains further that this teaching of God as *Sōtēr* is carried over into the New Testament with the references to God's common grace of causing the sun to rise on the evil and the good, sending rain on the just and the unjust, and being kind to even the unthankful and evil. The Scripture states, "In him we love and move and exist," and this is true of all mankind. Hendriksen continues:

He preserves, delivers, and in that sense saves, and that "saving" activity is by no means confined to the elect! On the voyage Dangerous (to Rome) God "saved" not only Paul but all those who were with him. There was no loss of life. Moreover, God also causes his gospel of salvation to be earnestly proclaimed to *all men*, that is, to men from every race and nation. Truly, the kindness of God extends to all. There is no one who does not in one way or another come within the reach of his benevolence. . . . This is really all that is needed in clarification of our present passage, 1 Tim 4:10.[23]

Hendriksen adds, "For not only is he a kind God, hence the *Sōtēr* (Preserver, Deliverer) of all men, showering blessings upon them, but he is in a very special sense the *Soter* (Savior) of those who by faith embrace him and his promise, for to them he imparts salvation, everlasting life in all its fullness."[24]

---

[23] Hendriksen, *Thessalonians, the Pastorals, and Hebrews*, NTC, 155–156.

[24] Hendriksen, *Thessalonians, the Pastorals, and Hebrews*, 156.

God is indeed the Savior of all men in a temporal sense as he allows them to continue living, demonstrates His kindness to them in blessings, and allows them to hear the glorious gospel of Christ. It is this understanding that Paul is bringing out in 1 Timothy 4:10, and is not speaking of God desiring all men to be saved; the statement in the text is not connected to any reference of Jesus's work of atonement at all. Robert Peterson and Michael Williams state, "This verse does not refer to Christ or his cross. Because Savior appears without qualification in 1 Timothy 4:10, it speaks of God the Father and not of Christ and thus is not a good proof text for unlimited atonement."[25] These texts are not contrary to unconditional, individual election, and are, therefore, have no basis for opposing this view.

Questions for Reflection

1. Do you agree that Peter uses first and second pronouns to refer to believers only?
2. According to the Arminian view, if God is not willing for any to perish, why are sinners still perishing?
3. Is God not willing for any of His elect to perish then?
4. Do you agree that 1 Timothy 2:4 is meaning all "kinds" of men?
5. Is God the Savior of all men salvifically? What is the implication of having that view?

---

[25] Robert A. Peterson and Michael D. Williams, *Why I'm Not an Arminian* (Downer Grove: IVP, 2004), 208.

Chapter Six
Love and Hate

"Misconceptions of the nature of God, an unbiblical conception of love, and fallen humanity's notions of fairness have caused many to balk at the idea that God unconditionally chooses some and not others to receive salvation."[1]

One of the most often quoted passages against unconditional election is John 3:16. This passage is the definitive "go-to" text for Arminian Christians. Much of the discussion revolves around the words "whoever" and "world" as if to mean that it is referring to any and every single individual in the entire world past, present, and future. It is my conviction that this passage is not at all a rebuttal against unconditional election, but simply makes statements of reality of those who come to Christ. We will spend some time exploring this passage used to oppose the Reformed view.

God So Loved the World (John 3:16)

This passage is one that most of us know by heart: "For God so loved the world that he gave His only begotten Son, that whoever believes in him shall not perish, but have eternal life." Again, this passage is used as a proof text to refute unconditional election; however, as we examine this verse we will see that it does not. This is not to say that John 3:16 is unimportant or lacks any theological depth. That would, indeed, be a mistake to view this beloved passage in this manner. As Burk Parsons stated, "John 3:16 is at the very foundation of Reformed theology. In John

---

[1] MacArthur and Mayhue, *Bible Doctrine*, 493.

3:16, we find every tenet of Reformed soteriology in its most basic form."[2] Charles Spurgeon commenting on this passage said, "John 3:16 might be put in the forefront of all my volumes of discourses as the sole topic of my life's ministry."[3] This passage cannot be diminished as to its overall importance in the Christian message of Christ.

The question, then, is not whether this text is to be regarded as insignificant or undeserving of serious attention, but whether or not the text refutes unconditional election. For many it certainly does. One writer says that "they [Arminian Christians] say this: 'God can't elect certain ones to salvation because John 3:16 says that God so loved the world. . . . Therefore, God has done His part in offering the gift of salvation in His Son and just leaves it up to us to receive the gift through faith. Amen. Case closed!'"[4] What do we say to this? We always go back to the context of the passage and allow the passage to interpret itself rather than us reading into the passage what is not there.

Looking at the context, then, Jesus is having a conversation with Nicodemus who is a ruler of the Jews (3:1). Nicodemus has come by night to speak with Jesus and our Lord immediately says to him, "Truly, truly, I say to you, unless one is born again he cannot see the kingdom of God" (3:3). Jesus says again, "Truly, truly I say to you, unless one is born of water and the Spirit, he cannot enter into the kingdom of God" (3:5). Our Lord is reminding Nicodemus of what was written in prior times through the prophet Ezekiel: "Then I will sprinkle clean water on you, and you will be clean; I will cleanse you from all your filthiness and from all your idols. Moreover, I will give you a new heart and put a new spirit within you; and I will remove the heart of stone from your flesh and give you a heart of flesh. I will put My Spirit within you and cause you to walk in My statutes, and you will be careful to ob-

---

[2] Burk Parsons, "Reformed Theology & John 3:16," *Ligonier*, April 25, 2016, https://www.ligonier.org/learn/articles/reformed-theology-john-316.

[3] Parsons, "Reformed Theology & John 3:16."

[4] John Samson, "What About John 3:16," Excerpt from *Twelve What Abouts*, https://www.monergism.com/what-about-john-316.

serve My ordinances" (Ezek 36:25–27). The Lord Jesus is explaining to Nicodemus of the regenerating work of the Holy Spirit of God. Before one can see or enter the kingdom—and we enter the kingdom and see the kingdom through faith—he or she must be born of the Spirit. Jesus then likens the working of the Holy Spirit to the wind: "The wind blows where it wishes and you hear the sound of it, but do not know where it comes from and where it is going; so is everyone who is born of the Spirit" (John 3:8). F. F. Bruce writes, "As the coming and going of the wind cannot be controlled by human power or wisdom, so the new birth of the Spirit is independent of human volition—coming neither 'from the will of flesh nor from the will of a man' as John has already put in his prologue (John 1:13). The hidden works of the Spirit in the human heart cannot be controlled or seen, but its effects are unmistakably evident."[5] The truth that Jesus establishes in these verses is that the new birth precedes the exercise of faith—as John also points out in 1:12–13—and that the Spirit of God moves upon people as he wills; the evidence of His work is their coming to faith.

As we then go further in Jesus's dialogue with Nicodemus, our Lord will begin to expound on His death for sinners. Jesus confirms His authority on these heavenly truths because it is he who descended from heaven, and then he states, "As Moses lifted up the serpent in the wilderness, even so must the Son of Man be lifted up, so that whoever believes will in him have eternal life" (John 3:14–15). This is the main statement of Jesus that is further detailed in verse 16. We read in verse 16, "For God so loved," which gives us the reason of why the Son of Man must be lifted up. The word "for" (gar) connects us to the preceding verse and gives explanation in addition to some other important words. Colin Kruse writes:

> The evangelist begins his comments with the much-loved words *For God so loved the world*. . . . Traditionally, the first

---

[5] F. F. Bruce, *The Gospel of John: Verse-By-Verse Exposition* (Nashville, TN: Kingsley Books), 125.

part of 3:16 has been interpreted so as to highlight the "degree" of God's love for the world, that is, "how much" he loved the world. . . . While it is true that the degree of God's love for the world was demonstrated by his giving his Son, this may not be what the evangelist is saying here. The word translated "so" (understood by many to mean "so much") is *houtōs*, a word used frequently elsewhere in the Gospel of John, but never to denote degree (how much) but always manner (in what way). Further, *houtōs* indicating "in what way" always refers back to something previously mentioned, not something about to be explained. Allowing these things to guide us, we would translate the first part of 3:16 as follows: "For in this way [referring to something already mentioned] God loved the world." An understanding of the way God loved the world would, then, be sought in the preceding verses, 3:14–15, where Jesus speaks of the Son of Man being "lifted up" just as the snake was lifted up on the pole by Moses, something God allowed to show his love for the world.[6]

Understanding this allows us to see the connection with verses 14–15 and how verse 16 is further explanation of those verses.

It is vital to understand also to whom Jesus is speaking. I say this because when Jesus makes known that God's love is for the world, this has great significance because of whom is being addressed. Jesus tells Nicodemus that "whoever" believes will have eternal life, and then we read in 3:16 that God loved the world. The mindset of the Jews in that day was that salvation was for them only, and Jesus expands God's love to include the world. Leon Morris writes, "The Jew was ready enough to think of God as loving Israel, but no passage appears to be cited in which any Jewish writer maintains that God loved the world. It is a distinctively Christian idea that God's love is wide enough to embrace

---

[6] Colin Kruse, *Gospel of John* TNTC (Downers Grove: InterVarsity Press, 2017), 116–17.

all people. His love is not confined to any national group or spiritual elite."[7] Köstenberger also writes, "Significantly, God's love extends not merely to Israel, but to the 'world,' that is sinful humanity."[8] This is great news for Gentiles—that God has extended His love and demonstrated that love by the giving of the Lord Jesus to be Lamb of God who takes away the sin of the world. D. A. Carson adds:

> From this survey it is clear that it is atypical for John to speak of God's love for the *world*, but this truth is therefore made to stand out as all the more wonderful. Jews were familiar with the truth that God loved the children of Israel; here God's love is not restricted by race. Even so, God's love is to be admired not because the world is so big and includes so many people, but because the world is so bad: that is the customary connotation of *kosmos*. The world is so wicked that John elsewhere forbids Christians to love it or anything in it. There is no contradiction between this prohibition and the fact that God does love it. Christians are not to love the world with the selfish love of participation; God loves the world with the selfless, costly love of redemption.[9]

The magnificence of John 3:16 is not the quantity of people God loved, but what kind of world he loved. Not only this, but the emphasis Jesus makes to Nicodemus is that this love that results in God sending His Only-Begotten Son not just for Israel but the nations! His love isn't restricted by race or ethnicity. Christ will purchase men from every tribe, tongue, people, and nation.

The other part of the debate lies in the word(s) "whoever" or "whosoever." The Arminian Christians emphasize this to point out, from their viewpoint, a universality of God's love and a uni-

---

[7] Leon Morris, *The Gospel According to John* (Grand Rapids: Eerdmans, 1995) 203.

[8] Andreas Köstenberger, *John,* BECNT (Grand Rapids: Baker Academic, 2004), 129.

[9] D. A. Carson, *The Gospel According to John,* PNTC (Grand Rapids: Eerdmans, 1991), 205.

versality of Christ's atonement. The text, however, does not emphasize that all people are in view or that Christ's atonement is for all. Actually, the text says nothing at all of the scope of Christ's redemptive work. This portion of John 3:16 in Greek reads, "*pas ho pisteuōn*," which means, "all the believing ones," or, "all the ones believing." The meaning, therefore, is all those who believe will not perish. The passage of John 3:16 says nothing about the extent of the atonement, whether God loves every single individual in existence, who can believe, or who will believe. The passage tells us that God loved the world, sinful humanity generally speaking, to the extent that he sent His Son to save the believing ones. Those who believe are the recipients of eternal life, and they will never perish. There is no more information given.

It is the other passages in the Gospel of John that give us that information. For example, John 1:12–13 and John 3:3–5 tell us that those who receive Christ, who are adopted by God, who enter and see the kingdom are those who were first born of him. In John 3:16, those who believe are those whom the Holy Spirit regenerates and brings to faith. This is in keeping with Jesus's words in John 6:37, 44, 65: "All that the Father gives Me will come to Me, and the one who comes to Me I will certainly not cast out. . . . No one can come to Me unless the Father who sent Me draws him; and I will raise him up on the last day. . . . For this reason I have said to you, that no one can come to Me unless it has been granted him from the Father."

John 3:16 also affirms God's love for the world. Is this salvific love? Is it the same degree of love toward believers and unbelievers? How are believers to understand God's love? Much of the debate between Reformed and Arminian theologians revolves around understanding the love of God. First John 4:8 affirms that "God is love." His love is truly seen in the salvific work of Christ as the Apostle Paul states in Romans 5:8: "But God demonstrates His own love toward us, in that while we were yet sinners, Christ died for us." These truths are not debated among Reformed and Arminian theologians. The debate is whether God salvifically loves all, or only certain individuals. Geisler states,

It is true that there is nothing in sinners that prompts God to save us. Rather, as rightly objected, justice must condemn us in our own sinfulness. However, it is also true that there is something in God that prompts him to save: His love. Since God is essentially omnibenevolent, he must try to save His fallen creatures. Therefore, God does not have to show love because we deserve it, but because His nature demands it. Love is not an arbitrary attribute of God, but is rooted in His necessary nature. Hence, if he is all-loving, then he must love all.[10]

For Geisler, there is an obligation for the Lord to be loving to all. However, if this is to be applied as Geisler states, then why is God not loving toward Satan and the fallen angels—if indeed His nature compels him to be loving to all? Satan and his demons are no less fallen creatures, but God's love is not demonstrated toward them.

Another example to consider is the differences of love between husbands and wives (Eph 5:22-25), and the command toward all believers to "love your enemies" (Matt 5:44). Are believers to love their spouses in the same way they love their enemies? Certainly not. For example, the covenant love husbands are to have toward their wives is a special, exclusive, intimate love that is not extended to someone other than their wives. The Scripture says, "So husbands ought also to love their own wives as their own bodies. He who loves his own wife loves himself; for no one ever hated his own flesh, but nourishes and cherishes it, just as Christ also does the church" (Eph 5:28-29). Therefore, no one could rightly argue that a husband who loves his own wife with an exclusive, covenant love is somehow disobeying the command to love all, because he does not love all in the same way as he does his wife.

God's love is not obligated to all in the same way. In contrast to Geisler's view of God's love, the Lord says to Israel in Deuteronomy 7:7-8, "The Lord did not set His love on you nor choose

---

[10] Norman Geisler, *Systematic Theology in One Volume* (Bloomington, MI: Bethany House Publishers, 2011), 825.

you because you were more in number than any of the peoples, for you were the fewest of all peoples, but because the Lord loved you and kept the oath which he swore to your forefathers, the Lord brought you out by a mighty hand and redeemed you from the house of slavery, from the hand of Pharaoh king of Egypt." The implication of the Lord's statements to Israel is that because the Lord set His love on them out of all the nations of the earth, then the nations of the earth did not receive the special, covenant love of God. His lovingkindness (covenant love) is set only on Israel.

Within the Scripture, there are different types of God's love toward mankind. Sproul writes,

> Historically, three different types of the love of God have been distinguished. The first is His love of benevolence. The second is His love of beneficence. The third is His love of complacency. All three of these are grounded in and flow out of the goodness of God.[11]

Sproul goes on to state of God's benevolent love:

> We see that the benevolent love of God refers to His goodwill toward His creatures. . . . The spectacular sound and light show that took place in the fields outside of Bethlehem on the night of Christ's birth included the angelic announcement of peace on earth and goodwill toward men. The incarnation was an expression of the goodwill of God, His benevolent love. Christ came into the world not only by the will of the Father but also by the goodwill of the Father.[12]

In other words, the benevolent love of God is understood in terms of God's attitude toward His creatures. There is a kind disposition of God toward all mankind.

This leads to God's love of beneficence. Not only does God have an attitude of kindness toward all His creatures, but God

---

[11] R. C. Sproul, *God's Love: How the Infinite God Cares for His Children* (Colorado Springs, CO: David C. Cook Distribution, 2012), 147.

[12] Sproul, *God's Love*, 147–48.

also demonstrates that love toward them with actions. For example, Jesus states in Matthew 5:45, "For he causes His sun to rise on the evil and the good, and sends rain on the righteous and the unrighteous." Sproul states, "When we experience a rain shower, we do not see the raindrops falling with personal discrimination. . . . The righteous and the wicked both need an umbrella. At the same time, the wicked farmer and the righteous farmer receive refreshment for their fields."[13]

This kindness of God is also referred to by Reformed theologians as God's "common grace." Berkhof writes:

> When we speak of "common grace," we have in mind either (a) those general operations of the Holy Spirit whereby he, without renewing the heart, exercises such a moral influence on man through His general or special revelation, that sin is restrained, order is maintained in social life, and civil righteousness is promoted; or, (b) those general blessings, such as rain and sunshine, food and drink, clothing and shelter, which God imparts to all men indiscriminately where and in what measure it seems good to him.[14]

Though not salvific grace, this "common grace" is bestowed upon all without discrimination, for all are undeserved of this grace or this type of God's love. All the necessities of life or existence is freely given by God, which demonstrates the kindness of God to all.

The third type of love is God's love of complacency. Sproul states, "In theological language, the term complacent is used more in line with its etymology than with its current state. The Latin root originally meant 'to please greatly.' In this sense, God's love of complacency means that he is greatly pleased with His children."[15] Sproul goes on to state, "His love of complacency reflects His love in the creature's redeemed state. . . . It is by His love of complacency that he will say to us, 'Well done, good and

---

[13] Sproul, *God's Love*, 161.

[14] Berkhof, *Systematic Theology*, 436.

[15] Sproul, *God's Love*, 164.

faithful servant'" (Matt 25:21).[16] This is God's love for those who have entered into the New Covenant through faith in Christ Jesus. God's love of complacency is God's covenant love for those in Christ. It is not a general love or kindness toward all, but is an exclusive love for His redeemed.

This covenant love is now extended to include all who are brought into the New Covenant rather than exclusively the nation of Israel under the Old Covenant. Of the Gentiles the Apostle Paul says in Romans 9:25, "As he says also in Hosea, 'I will call those who were not My people, My people, and her who was not beloved, beloved.'" The Apostle John states in 1 John 3:1, "See how great a love the Father has bestowed on us, that we would be called children of God; and such we are. For this reason the world does not know us, because it did not know him." God's love is understood even greater when we see His love being granted to sinners on the basis of nothing else than His prerogative to grant it to whom he desires. When believers can understand God's covenant love as the writers of Scripture do, then His love is amplified to a higher degree more so than the kind of general love for all that Geisler presents. This understanding effects our obedience to him, our confidence in him, our praise to him, our desire to be more like him, and our humility before him. God's special love is more fully known when contemplating the Reformed doctrine of election.

Jacob I Loved (Romans 9:11–13)

In light of God's love, how are we to understand God's hate? If we say that God only loves His people with that special, covenant love, then the implication is that everyone else is excluded from that love, and receive God's hate. This is abominable to Arminians who maintain God's love is to all equally, however, the Scripture records God's hate of individuals. If we can understand this text correctly, it produces in us a greater appreciation for

---

[16] Sproul, God's Love, 165.

being the recipients of God's love in view of the fact that he is not obligated to give it to any.

In the passage of Romans 9:11–13, Arminian theologians seek to interpret the phrase, "Jacob I hated," to not mean "hate" but simply that God preferred Jacob over Esau. This is their attempt, as stated above, to maintain God's universal love to all equally. Reformed theologians often refer to Romans 9 to demonstrate the doctrine of election because that chapter expounds it directly. Used by Arminian adherents as a proof-text for their position, Klein states with reference to verse thirteen:

> As God had named or counted Abraham's seed through Isaac (9:7), so now the line would run through Jacob, not Esau. This choice of what was to become Israel's lineage was a sovereign act, not motivated by any specific acts or responses from the twins. This was God's sovereign choice, though we hasten to add that the issue here is not Jacob or Esau's personal salvation.[17]

Richard Hardin writes that in Romans 9 the Apostle Paul taught on election to service and not to salvation.[18] He goes on to point out how the Lord blessed the life of Esau and states, "Did God hate Esau? No! God helped Esau capture his homeland during the twenty years Jacob was working for his wives and cattle."[19] This same view is echoed by Geisler when he states, "God is not speaking here about the individual Jacob but about the nation of Jacob (Israel)."[20] In other words, the text of Romans 9:11–13 is not speaking of Jacob and Esau as individuals, nor of salvation of either. The emphasis, according to the above men, is that God chose the people of Israel for service rather than the descendants of Esau.

---

[17] Klein, *New Chosen People*, 145.

[18] Richard Hardin, *God Loved Esau: Predestination and Election is to Service-Not Salvation* (CreateSpace Independent Publishing Platform, 2010), 12.

[19] Hardin, *God Loved Esau*, 11.

[20] Geisler, *Chosen but Free*, 83.

The question of whether God actually hated Esau or rather that he simply chose Jacob over Esau for service centers on the meaning of "hated." Geisler states that "hated" really means "loved less." To validate this meaning he cites the passage in Genesis 29:30–31 where it is said that Jacob loved Rachel more than Leah: "The Lord saw that Leah was hated." Geisler also cites Jesus's words in Luke 14:26 as proof that "hate," means, "loved less": "If anyone comes to Me, and does not hate his own father and mother and wife and children and brothers and sisters, yes, and even his own life, he cannot be My disciple." It is important to note that Luke 14:26 is the parallel passage of Matthew 10:37, which reads, "He who loves father or mother more than Me is not worthy of Me; and he who loves son or daughter more than Me is not worthy of Me." Hendriksen writes, "That the word hate in Luke 14:26 cannot have the meaning which we generally attach to it is clear also from the fact that Jesus tells us to love even our enemies (Matt 5:44). Then we should certainly love and not hate members of our immediate family."[21] The Lord is demanding from His disciples a complete loyalty to him "that is so true and unswerving that every other attachment, even that to one's own life, must be subjected to it."[22] It is apparent in Luke 14:26 that Jesus is not actually commanding His people to hate or loathe their family. In this passage the meaning is indeed "love less." However, the primary use of this word in the New Testament does not mean "loved less" but rather "to hate." The Greek verb that is translated "hate" is *miseo*. Mounce defines the term as, "hating or having malicious feelings toward things or people."[23]

Interestingly, when one looks at a Greek concordance and examines all the Scriptures where *miseo* is used (37 times), it is clearly understood that in every other instance, aside from Luke 14:26, this word means "to hate or have malicious feelings toward." For example, Jesus says in Matthew 10:22, "You will be

---

[21] William Hendriksen, *Luke*, NTC (Grand Rapids: Baker, 2007), 735.

[22] Hendriksen, *Luke*, NTC, 735.

[23] Mounce, *Complete Expository of Old and New Testament Words*, 322.

hated by all because of My name, but it is the one who has endured to the end who will be saved." Of course, Jesus does not
mean that all will simply love the disciples less, but rather will
have malicious feelings toward them, and this is the meaning in
every use in Matthew's gospel. This is true in every other instance, and this includes the Apostle Paul's uses of this word elsewhere in Romans. He states of "slanderers, haters of God, inso-
lent, arrogant, boastful, inventors of evil, disobedient to parents"
(Rom 1:30), and states, "For what I am doing, I do not understand;
for I am not practicing what I would like to do, but I am doing the
very thing I hate" (Rom 7:15). In light of all the uses of this Greek
word in the New Testament, and its use in Romans, the plain
meaning of this Greek word is "to hate, to have malicious feelings
toward" rather than simply meaning, "loved less." Schreiner
writes,

> The words "I loved Jacob, but I hated Esau" are an exact ren-
> dition of the LXX, except that the object now precedes the
> verb, perhaps to emphasize that Jacob was the object of God's
> choice. The shocking nature of the verb "I hated" (*emisesa*) is
> sometimes explained in terms of the Semitic contrast be-
> tween "love" and "hate," so that the latter means "to love
> less." Even if this option is correct, which is doubtful here, it
> hardly lessens the problem, for the point of the text is that
> God set his affectionate love on Jacob and withheld it from
> Esau. It is a doubtful expedient in any case, since Malachi de-
> scribes God's "hatred" of Esau (Edom) in active terms: he lays
> waste their land (Mal 1:3), tears down their buildings (v. 4),
> and his "anger" is on them "forever" (v. 4). What Romans 9:13
> adds to the promise of verse 12 is that the submission of the
> older to the younger is based on God's choice of Jacob and his
> rejection of Esau.[24]

In other words, even if the text is speaking about the nations of
Israel and Edom, the meaning of God's hatred toward Esau

---

[24] Schreiner, *Romans*, BECNT, 797.

(Edom) is still present and explained further by God's actions toward them.

Despite the views expounded by Geisler and others, the text of Romans 9:11–13 is speaking of Jacob and Esau as individuals. Hendriksen writes in opposition to the view that Jacob and Esau represent two nations: "Though it is true that in Genesis 25:22, 23 the text turns quickly from babes to nations, nevertheless the starting point has to do with persons, not nations."[25] He adds that the Malachi context is similar and says, "Here too the starting point is certainly personal: 'Was not Esau Jacob's brother . . . yet I loved Jacob but Esau I hated.' Paul had every right, therefore, to apply these passages to persons, as he did."[26] Lawson sums up the intent of this passage and states, "Often misperceived as a harsh teaching that portrays a cruel, despotic God, the doctrine of election actually is a doctrine of amazing love."[27] Lawson adds, "It is the truth of God's special love for His chosen ones, a sovereign love that is eternal, unconditional, and immutable."[28] The text of Romans 9:11–13 strongly suggests that individuals are in view rather than nations as Hendriksen points out. Hodges also writes in support of this view:

> It is clear that this distinction between the two races presupposed and included a distinction between the individuals. Jacob was made the special heir to his father Isaac, obtained as an individual the birthright and the blessing, and Esau as an individual was cast off. The one, therefore, was personally preferred to the other. In Paul's application of this event to his argument, the distinction between the two as individuals was the very thing referred to. This is plain from the 11th verse, in which he says, "The children being not yet born,

[25] Hendriksen, *Romans*, NTC, 323.
[26] Hendriksen, *Romans*, NTC, 323.
[27] Lawson, *Foundations of Grace*, vol. 1, 353.
[28] Lawson, *Foundations of Grace*, vol. 1, 353.

neither having done any good or evil." It is, therefore, the nature of the choice between the children that is the point designed to be presented.[29]

As Cottrell stated earlier, one cannot affirm corporate election while denying individual election.[30] The Scripture affirms that Esau was a godless and immoral person (Heb 12:16), and also "that no immoral or impure person or covetous man, who is an idolater, has an inheritance in the kingdom of Christ and God" (Eph 5:5). In view of the text of Romans 9:11–13, the Lord's affection for Jacob was not extended to Esau. Fesko states:

> Only by God's sovereign election did Jacob, a deceiver and a conniver, receive God's covenant blessings. By contrast, even though Esau physically descended from Isaac, the Scriptures characterize him very differently—he was "a fornicator" and "profane," someone who sold his interest in God's covenant promises and who would eventually fall under God's righteous judgement (Gen 27:39–40; Jer 49:8–10; Obad 8–9, 18–19; Mal 1:1–4). Before the foundation of the world, God set His love on Jacob and chose him so that he would be called, justified, and glorified. By contrast, God did not set His love on Esau. With God there is no middle ground—God is not indifferent toward people. He either loves or hates them. And by hate we should recognize that God's hatred is holy and pure, unlike our own sinful manifestations of hatred.[31]

The text of Romans 9:11–13 emphasizes the reality of God's election of individuals and His rejection of individuals that is grounded in "God's purpose according to His choice," which is not according to any merit foreseen. After all, Paul states it definitely: "Not because of works but because of him who calls" (Rom 9:11). There are no prior conditions that can be met for God to

---

[29] Charles Hodges, *Commentary on the Epistle to the Romans* Philadelphia: Grigg and Elliot, 1835), 391.

[30] Cottrell, "Classical Arminian View," 80.

[31] J. V. Fesko, *Romans*, LC (Grand Rapids: Reformation Heritage Books, 2018), 257–58.

elect any to faith, but as the apostle writes, "It does not depend on the man who wills or the man who runs, but on God who has mercy" (Rom 9:16). It is understood by these truths that those who are the recipients of God's unconditional love are blessed beyond measure. God was never obligated to extend love to any, and yet he does so through Christ Jesus. God could have left us in our sin and continued to have been the recipients of His righteous hate, but grace has been extended to those whom he chose to extend it to. God does not love all equally, but only those in Christ, who are in him because of His sovereign, free choice to save whom he desires. Having, then, a correct view of God's love and hate from Scripture, which supports the Reformed position of election, we may now begin to explore the relationship between election and sanctification.

Questions for Reflection

1. Is John 3:16 a proof text against unconditional election?
2. Does "world" always imply every single individual in the world?
3. What does John 3:16 teach about election or the extent of the atonement?
4. Is God obligated to love everyone equally?
5. Which view of election is most consistent with the teaching of Scripture in your view?

Section III

Election and Sanctification

Chapter Seven
To the Praise of His Glory

"The doctrine of election does increase praise given to God for our salvation and seriously diminishes any pride that we might feel if we thought that our salvation was due to something good in us or something for which we should receive credit."[1]

The doctrine of election is a fascinating doctrine, to be sure, because it is in this teaching that the Scriptures declare that the people of God are chosen by God unto salvation. Sadly, it seems that this glorious topic is delegated to the section of the Christian life that is left to theologians to debate among themselves. In my experience, when this topic is raised between me and other believers, the general response I receive is, "Why does this matter anyway?" This is one of the great tragedies that has fallen upon the church in our day concerning deep doctrinal subjects; deep theology is reserved for the scholars, and ordinary Christians do not need to worry themselves with these issues. The Scriptures, however, place the doctrine of election within the experience of the everyday believer and as a vital part of his Christian life. Interestingly, even the heretic Clark Pinnock—no friend to evangelical orthodoxy—stated, "How we handle divine election will say a lot about our vision of Christianity as a whole."[2]

What we believe about this doctrine affects us in the area of our sanctification, and therefore, is for all of us to know and study. This is evidenced even by the simple fact that when the Apostle Paul writes to the church of Ephesus or Rome, he does not speak only to scholars and theologians but to all within those

---

[1] Wayne Grudem, *Systematic Theology*, 674.

[2] Clark Pinnock, "Divine Election as Corporate, Open, and Vocational," in *Perspectives on Election,* Edited by Chad Owen Brand (Nashville: B&H Academic, 2006), 278.

churches. It is from these two epistles, especially, that we receive much of our understanding of the doctrine of election.

The purpose of section 3 is to expound several passages that reference the doctrine of election, and to demonstrate that these passages are intimately linked with sanctification. For example, the Apostle Paul states in Ephesians 1:4, "just as he chose us in him before the foundation of the world, that we would be holy and blameless before him." The apostle also says in Colossians 3:12, "So, as those who have been chosen of God, holy and beloved, put on a heart of compassion, kindness, humility, gentleness and patience." In these two verses, along with the others that will be expounded, election and sanctification are clearly linked together. The implication of this truth is that the biblical doctrine of election is intended to bring about certain results in our sanctification when it is correctly understood. These numerous aspects of our sanctification are surely present in genuine, committed believers who are not Reformed, but the degree to which these aspects are cultivated in the lives of believers will be greater. When we ignore or misunderstand this doctrine, we will inevitably fall short of the potential of greater growth in Christlikeness.

A Reason to Praise God (Ephesians 1:3-6)

In Ephesians chapter 1, we read of this marvelous reality of our election in Christ before the foundation of the world (v. 4). This passage was referenced in the previous section, but its full implication is to be discussed here. It is in the beginning of this epistle that we understand that the doctrine of election is given to stir praise within our hearts to God. This is evident in Paul's opening words regarding the Father who has blessed His people. Bryan Chapell states, "Praise of our Father is really the focus of the passage. The apostle says that we should praise God, because he blesses us as our Father."[3] The Apostle Paul writes in Ephesians 1:3-6:

---

[3] Chapell, *Ephesians*, REC, 18.

Blessed be the God and Father of our Lord Jesus Christ, who has blessed us with every spiritual blessing in the heavenly places in Christ, just as he chose us in him before the foundation of the world, that we would be holy and blameless before him. In love he predestined us to adoption as sons through Jesus Christ to himself, according to the kind intention of His will, to the praise of the glory of His grace, which he freely bestowed on us in the Beloved.

In response, the sixteenth-century Reformer John Calvin writes, "The lofty terms, in which he extolls the grace of God toward the Ephesians, are intended to rouse their hearts to gratitude, to set them all on flame, to fill them even to overflowing with this thought."[4] The passage is designed, as Calvin states, "to assert the riches of divine grace toward the Ephesians."[5] Frank Thielman writes,

> The verbal adjective *eulogetos*... means "blessed" in the sense of "praised," and therefore Paul is saying that God is praised by those whom he has blessed. He is not expressing the wish that God would be blessed or issuing an implicit admonition that he should be blessed, but in a way analogous to his brief benediction in Rom 1:25, Paul is saying that God is blessed and implying that the people whom he blesses are those who bless him.[6]

The apostle's intention, then, is to praise the Father and call the readers to praise the Father also because he has blessed His people with "every spiritual blessing in the heavenly places in Christ" (v. 3). After this call to praise the Lord for His blessings, the apostle begins to expound those blessings in order to arouse within the people of God greater adoration for His glorious grace (v. 6). Thielman writes that "God has blessed believers not only because he chose them but also 'inasmuch as' or 'to the extent

---

[4] John Calvin, *Ephesians*, CC (Grand Rapids: Baker Books, 2009), 196.

[5] Calvin, *Ephesians*, CC, 196.

[6] Thielman, *Ephesians*, BECNT, 83.

that' he has given them these blessings in all their extrava-
gance."[7]

Blessed in Christ

The blessings of God, according to Paul, are "spiritual blessings" from the "heavenly places in Christ" (v. 3). These blessings
are described as "spiritual" (*pneumatikos*), meaning, "pertaining
or relating to the influences of the Holy Spirit."[8] Thielman states,
"When Paul uses the adjective *pneumatikos*... God's Spirit almost
always stands in the background."[9] Thielman goes on to say,
"'Spiritual blessings,' therefore, are the benefits that come as
gracious gifts from the Spirit of God and that Paul describes in
1:4–14."[10] These blessings are applied to the believer by the Spirit
of God, and as such originate from "the heavenly places" (v. 3).
Bruce writes, "Spiritual blessings are those which are appropri-
ate to people who have their true home in the heavenly realm."[11]
The Holy Spirit applies these blessings to the elect of God.

The phrase "in Christ" expresses the union between Christ
and His people. Hendriksen writes, "[The phrase, 'In Christ'] or
its equivalent occurs more than ten times in this short paragraph
(1:3–14), [and is] clear evidence of the fact that the apostle regarded Christ as the very foundation of the church, that is, of all
its benefits, of its complete salvation."[12] Bruce further states,
"The writer and his readers are 'in Christ'—members of Christ,
sharers of his resurrection-life—and because Christ himself is
now exalted in the heavenly realm, those who are 'in him' belong
to that heavenly realm, too, in the mind of God."[13] It is Father who

---

[7] Thielman, *Ephesians*, BECNT, 86.

[8] Mounce, *Analytical Lexicon to the Greek New Testament*, 380.

[9] Thielman, *Ephesians*, BECNT, 84.

[10] Thielman, *Ephesians*, BECNT, 84.

[11] F. F. Bruce, *The Epistle to the Ephesians: A Verse-by-Verse Exposition* (Bath, UK: Creative Communications Ltd, 2012), 19.

[12] Hendriksen, *Ephesians*, NTC, 74.

[13] Bruce, *Ephesians*, 19.

has blessed the people of God with blessings applied by the Spirit of God as a result of their union with the Lord Jesus.

The first blessing that the apostle speaks of to the church of Ephesus is God's choosing them unto salvation. Thielman states:

> Paul begins his description of God's blessings by saying that God "chose us" (*exelexato hēmas*). . . . Paul considers God's free choice of his people to be the clearest indicator of the lavish nature of his grace, as the frequent repetition of the theme of God's gracious initiative in blessing his people shows.[14]

The word "chose" (*exelexato*) means, "to select someone/something for oneself."[15] Because this Greek word is in the aorist middle indicative, the meaning conveyed by Paul is that "he chose us for himself."[16] The blessing of God's selecting individuals was accomplished "before the foundation of the world" (v. 4). Bruce states the following:

> So far as the personal experience of believers is concerned, their entry into the relationship described by the words "in Christ" took place when they were born from above . . . but from God's point of view it has no such temporal limitation. They have been the objects of his eternal choice, and that eternal choice is so completely bound up with the person of Christ that in the light of the divine purpose they are described as being "in Christ" before the world's foundation.[17]

In other words, before the Lord ever created anything, he chose individuals unto salvation through the work of the Lord Jesus.

---

[14] Thielman, *Ephesians*, BECNT, 86.

[15] Benjamin Merkle, *Ephesians*, EGGNT (Nashville: B&H Academic, 2016), 38.

[16] Merkle, *Ephesians*, EGGNT, 38.

[17] Bruce, *Ephesians*, 19.

Corporate, Conditional, or Unconditional?

As stated earlier, theologians/interpreters advocate different views of the doctrine of election. This is demonstrated by their understanding of the text of Ephesians 1:3–6. For example, Klein states,

> Paul sees the entire body of Christ as the object of God's pretemporal election. This is not to deny that election is personal: certainly every member of the church shares in its election. Paul does not, however, assert here particular or individual election, i. e., that God has selected specific individuals for inclusion in the church. He underscores the church's corporate election in Christ, who is God's elect one (Luke 9:35; 23:35). Being incorporated in Christ, the church attains its identity, all of its blessings and its chosen position. God devised this strategy to bless the church in Christ even before he created the world.[18]

In other words, Klein views election as purely corporate in nature and the only elect individual is Christ, the elect One. He goes on to state, "By predestination in his various uses, Paul asserts that God determined ahead of time certain states of affairs: that he conform believers to Christ's image, that wisdom achieve the glory of his people, and that we be for the praise of his glory."[19] For Klein, God has not determined the salvation of individuals, the means of them entering into the body of Christ, or that some would have faith while others would not.[20] In other words, God determined that the body of Christ, who are in the Elect One, would receive the benefits of salvation.

---

[18] William Klein, *Ephesians*, EBC (Grand Rapids: Zondervan, 2006), 71.

[19] Klein, *Ephesians*, EBC, 72.

[20] Klein, *Ephesians*, EBC, 73.

Regarding how sinners enter the body of Christ to receive God's predetermined benefits, Klein states that God's foreknowledge is the basis for His determination to bless corporately those are in Christ.[21] He states his position saying:

> What God knows about his plans and purposes for his people does not violate the requirement that they exercise faith that saves . . . Paul declares that God elected and predetermined a destiny for his people in full knowledge of what they were, what they would be without his intervention, and, most significantly what they would become as the result of his grace on their behalf. God knows them thoroughly, even before they existed as a people: this is his foreknowledge.[22]

In other words, Klein takes the Arminian position that God simply foreknows who will believe and predetermined that those who exercised faith would be blessed. In opposition to Klein's view that Paul's intent in Ephesians 1 is only to show the corporate nature of election, Clinton Arnold writes:

> The principal reason for the praise is that "he [God] chose us" (exelexato). This term was commonly used in the LXX for God's choice of individuals: He chose Abraham (Neh 9:7), Aaron (Ps 105:26 [104:26], Moses (Sirach 45:4), David (1 Kings 11:34; Ps 78:70 [77:70]), and Eli's father (1 Sam 2:28). Most importantly, he chose Jacob/Israel (Isa 41:8; 44:1–2) to set his love upon him and his descendants (Deut 7:7; 10:15) and for Jacob to be his own special possession (14:2). The verb is also used to speak of God's choosing Christ. When God spoke from the cloud at the scene of the transfiguration, he said, "This is my Son, whom I have chosen; listen to him" (Luke 9:35). The latter case, of course, does not mean that God has chosen Christ to experience redemption and the forgiveness of sins

---

[21] Klein, *The New Chosen People,* 134.

[22] Klein, *The New Chosen People,* 136.

as is in view for the elect here, but that he chose Christ to fulfill a particular and indispensable role for securing salvation.

The usage of the verb suggests that God chooses individuals and together they comprise the group ("us"; *hēmas*). Throughout this letter there is an oscillation between the individual and the group. In the ethical exhortation of chapters 4–6, Paul addresses the group ("you"; second person plural), but implicit with each admonition is the personal responsibility of each individual member of the group. Thus, when he admonishes them to "speak truth" (4:25), "be kind" (4:32), or "walk in love" (5:2) using the second person plural, each individual is expected to receive this as a command directly to him or her and to bring their conduct in line with these virtues. At times, Paul can make this more explicit, such as when he says "speak truth, each one of you" (4:25), but this is for emphasis. An individual application is present with each second person plural exhortation.[23]

Arnold points out that the corporate group who receives the benefits Paul speaks of does not nullify the individual emphasis of the reality of election. The apostle's exhortations throughout the rest of the epistle are toward the individuals who make up the church. Arnold goes on to state, "Paul is affirming that his believing readers have been chosen by God, but he is not denying that God has individually chosen them to be in a relationship with himself, as the choice of the verb (*exelexato*) strongly suggests."[24]

God's Unconditional Selection

It is the Reformed theologian's conviction that God's act of election is individual and unconditional. Though some such as Arminian William Klein affirm only corporate election and that

---

[23] Clinton E. Arnold, *Ephesians*, ECNT (Grand Rapids: Zondervan, 2010), 101–102.
[24] Arnold, *Ephesians*, ECNT, 102.

Christ is the only individual elect of God, the text of Ephesians 1:4 details the saints as the object of God's election, not Christ. The saints are elected to be holy and blameless (v. 4), and the saints are adopted by the Father (v. 5). The teaching of election in this passage is not simply corporate, but individuals are implied as well. Arnold writes, "Individual election is also necessitated by the metaphor of adoption that he uses two lines later. In the Roman world, groups were not adopted by a *paterfamilias*, only individuals."[25] Therefore, in keeping with Paul's analogy of individual adoption, and his use of the word *exelexato* (used of individuals in the LXX as Arnold points out[26]), the text strongly implies individual election.

The election of God taught in Ephesians 1:3–14 is not said to be the result of foreseen faith (this will be discussed later in this chapter), but of an act of God's kindness: "according to the kind intention of His will" (v. 5). This is more in line with unconditional election. Bruce Ware states that this unconditional election from God refers to the claim that God's selection of those he would save is not based upon or conditioned by any fact or feature of those persons or anything they would do, or any choice they would make.[27] This is vitally important to understand in view of this passage. The Apostle Paul states, "In love he predestined us to adoption as sons through Jesus Christ to himself according to the kind intention of His will" (v. 5). Thielman states, "Paul's focus is not on the logic of election but on its occurrence

---

[25] Arnold, *Ephesians*, ECNT, 102.

[26] Arnold, *Ephesians*, ECNT, 101.

[27] Ware, "Divine Election to Salvation," 2. Ware writes, "Unconditional election refers to the claim that God's selection of those whom He would save was not based upon (or, not 'conditioned' on) some fact or feature of those individuals' lives, in particular. That is, God's election of those who would be saved was not conditioned on something they would do, some choice they would make, how good or bad they might be, or anything else specifically true about them in contrast to others also enslaved to sin deserving God's just condemnation."

and the need to praise God because his choice of a people for himself is such a clear demonstration of his grace."[28] Thielman goes on to write:

> Paul's use of language in Ephesians generally, and in this benediction particularly, moreover, is as lavish in its own way as the grace of God, which he praises. Redundancy, then, is not a valid objection to understanding *proorisas hēmas* (predestined us) as a restatement of *exelexato hēmas* (chose us). Paul simply turns the jewel slightly and views it from a different angle, now describing God's primordial action on behalf of his people not as his choice but as his predetermination of them. God determined that they would be his people before the foundation of the world. Their status as his people, therefore, came as an utterly free gift, irrespective of anything they could possibly have done to merit it.[29]

Carl Trueman states that God's election is an election of grace. He adds that God chose Abram, not because he was impressive or influential, but rather because God decided to choose him and not another. He writes, "The decision to choose Abraham was not based on intrinsic merit or foreseen faith but solely on the Lord's will and His gracious plan."[30] As with Abraham, the Lord, for example, expressed this truth to Abraham's descendants in Deuteronomy 7:7–8:

> The Lord did not set His love on you nor choose you because you were more in number than any of the peoples, for you were fewest of all peoples, but because the Lord loved you

---

[28] Thielman, *Ephesians*, BECNT, 91.

[29] Thielman, *Ephesians*, BECNT, 91.

[30] Carl Trueman, *Grace Alone: Salvation as a Gift of God* (Grand Rapids: Zondervan, 2017), 41–42. He writes, "This election is of grace. God does not call Abram because he is particularly impressive or influential figure. He calls him simply because he decides to choose him and not another (Gen 12:1–3; Isa 51:2). The decision to choose Abraham was not based on intrinsic merit or foreseen faith but solely on the Lord's will and his gracious plan. God often reminded Abraham's descendants that their election was an act of sovereign grace."

and kept the oath which he swore to your forefathers, the Lord brought you out by a mighty hand and redeemed you from the house of slavery, from the hand of the Pharaoh, king of Egypt.

He did not choose them because they were great in number but simply chose to bestow His love upon them out of all the nations of the earth.

The Apostle Paul uses similar language in Romans 9 when speaking Jacob and Esau: "For though the twins were not yet born and had not done anything good or bad, so that God's purpose according to His choice would stand, not because of works but of him who calls." God's choice of Israel was not according to anything "special in them" and God's choice of Jacob over Esau was not because of anything that he foresaw in either, whether good or bad, but solely according to His choice. For those chosen of God, there are no qualities, actions, or choices whereby the Holy One would be obligated or persuaded to grant His salvation to sinful, unregenerate rebels. He does so by a pure act of grace, and it is this reality that is being taught in Ephesians 1. Lawson states that the Father chose His elect, all whom he purposed to save, long before the creation of all things, and did so not based on anything he foresaw in them, but simply on His good pleasure.[31] The Father has "blessed" (*eulogeo*) us in Christ. Hendriksen states that "the Father blesses His children when he lavishes gifts upon them in His favor so that these bounties or these experiences, of whatever nature, work together for their good. Together with the gift he imparts himself."[32] The reality being expounded by the Apostle Paul is that God chose unto salvation a people who were not deserving of any mercy because they were inherently good, but rather they were underserving of God's salvation, and yet he bestowed salvific gifts upon them: election, redemption, forgiveness, and certification as children of God.

---

[31] Lawson, *Foundations of Grace*, 417.

[32] Hendriksen, *Ephesians*, NTC, 73.

Elected to be Holy and Blameless

One of the results of God's election of sinners unto salvation is that they would be "holy and blameless before him" (v. 4). The implication, then, was that we were not in and of ourselves—specifically, holy and blameless. The word "holy" refers to the "process of making pure or holy."[33] The implication, then, is that men, in their natural state, are not holy and blameless, and are, in fact, haters of God. The Scripture states in Romans 8:6–7, "For the mind set on the flesh is death . . . because the mind set on the flesh is hostile toward God; for it does not subject itself to the law of God, for it is not even able to do so." The natural state of man is that of wickedness, walking in darkness and hostility toward the Holy One. Again, the apostle states in Romans 5:12, "Therefore, just as through one man sin entered into the world, and death through sin, and so death spread to all men, because all sinned." Augustine writes, "Human nature was in his [Adam's] person vitiated and altered to such an extent that he suffered in his members the warring of disobedient lust, and became subject to the necessity of dying. And what he himself had become by sin and punishment, such he passed down to those whom he generated."[34] In other words, when Adam sinned against the Lord, his nature changed from that of being in a state of innocence to that of being in rebellion with an inclination for continued rebellion. Jesus says in John 3:20, "For everyone who does evil hates the Light." This natural state was then passed to all mankind. Because of the Fall, mankind's affection for God was lost whereby men love darkness rather than the Light because their deeds are evil (John 3:19). However, as a result of God's work of regeneration, the Scripture states, "Therefore if anyone is in Christ, he is a new creature; the old things passed away; behold new things have come" (2 Cor 5:17).

---

[33] Mounce, *Complete Expository Dictionary of Old and New Testament Words*, 338.

[34] Cited in Greg Allison, *Historical Theology: An Introduction to Christian Doctrine* (Grand Rapids: Zondervan, 2011), 348.

As new creations, our minds, wills, and affections have been changed to desire, love, and glorify Christ. Though the view of some is that God foresaw faith and elected sinners on that basis, there is, however, no good in them, no holiness or righteousness that would ever prompt the desire to come to him. The teaching of "prevenient grace" does not satisfy the dilemma of why sinners come to Christ because, first off, this teaching is absent in Scripture, and secondly, this teaching does not take into account the severe state of rebellion that man is in naturally. All human beings are "dead in trespasses and sins: (Eph 2:1) and are "by nature children of wrath" (Eph 2:3). As stated earlier, the unregenerate man is not able to subject his mind, that is set on the flesh, to the law of God (Rom 8:7). Paul adds, "It [the mind set on the flesh] is not even able to do so" (Rom 8:7).

The Apostle Paul states in Acts 17:30, "God is now declaring to men that all people everywhere should repent." This is a command of God, and as such, part of the law of God. But as has just been noted, Paul states that those in the flesh do not subject themselves to the law of God (Rom 8:7). Therefore, even if one promotes the idea of prevenient grace, it does not provide an explanation of how an unregenerate man, even in a state of neutrality (though neutrality does not exist), can choose to obey God's command to repent. MacArthur and Mayhue write that the idea behind prevenient grace is that it "removes the effects of depravity for everyone, bringing all men into a state of neutrality by which they can accept or reject Christ."[35] A state of supposed neutrality does give an unregenerate man, who is by nature a child of wrath, the ability to subject his still fleshly mind to the law of God. It is only because of the Spirit's work of regeneration that a sinner comes before God holy and blameless to obey him. Hendriksen states, "It is worthy of special note that Paul does not say, 'The Father elected us because he foresaw that we were going to be holy," but rather, "that we should be holy."[36] The implication, then, is that if God saved us to be holy, then apart from

---

[35] MacArthur and Mayhue, *Biblical Doctrine*, 555.

[36] Hendriksen, *Ephesians*, NTC, 77.

His work we are not holy and blameless, but unholy, dead, guilty, and hostile toward God.

Changing our Affections

God's purpose, according to the apostle, in electing a people unto himself was to remove their blame, grant to them the forgiveness of sins, and seal them with the Holy Spirit of promise which would then result in the regenerated people glorifying God. However, as John Calvin writes, holiness is the immediate, but not chief, design of election. He states, "Holiness, purity, and every excellence that is found among men, are the fruit of salvation," and adds that the highest end of this work of God is the glory of God.[37] The act of God's work in regeneration results in His work of sanctification, which includes changing our affections for the Lord. Thomas Watson stated, "After the fall, the affections were misplaced on wrong objects; in sanctification, they are turned into a sweet order and harmony, the grief placed on sin, the love of God, the joy on heaven."[38] Similarly, Tony Reinke writes,

> Regeneration is the awakening and enlivening of the spiritual heart, and sanctification is the ongoing work of recalibrating the affections to cherish what God cherishes. And because we are becoming like what we worship, this is a critical work of grace in our hearts. Sanctification is more than saying "no" to sin. Sanctification says "yes" to holiness and glad

---

[37] Calvin, *Ephesians*, CC, 198–99. He writes, "This is the immediate design, but not the chief design; for there is no absurdity in supposing that the same things may gain two objects. The design of the building is, that there should be a house. This is the immediate design, but the convenience of dwelling in it is the ultimate design. It was necessary to mention this in passing; for we shall immediately find that Paul mentions another design, the glory of God. But there is no contradiction here; for the glory of God is the highest end, to which our sanctification is subordinate" (199).

[38] Thomas Watson, *A Body of Divinity* (Zeeland, MI: Reformed Church Publications, 2009), 264.

obedience to Jesus. Sanctification says yes to loving God and what he loves. Sanctification is all about retraining our delights.[39]

It is in the work of sanctification that the affections of the Christian are drawn toward Christ—to love him, to commit to him, and to praise him.

The obedience rendered to Christ is not out of "duty" but out of genuine affection for him after having been regenerated by the Spirit of God. The affections of the sinful heart that was hostile toward God is replaced with love and commitment to Christ. John Flavel states, "Sanctification gives sin a miscarrying womb after it has conceived in the soul."[40] The work of sanctification is a process of undoing the effects of sin and the Fall and making God and Christ the focus of love and desire. The psalmist writes in Psalm 42:1, "As the deer pants for the water brooks, so my soul pants for You, O God." Asaph writes in Psalm 73:25, "Whom have I in heaven but You? And besides You, I desire nothing on earth." Psalm 103:1–3 states: "Bless the Lord, O my soul, and all that is within me, bless His holy name. Bless the Lord, O my soul, and forget none of His benefits: who pardons all your iniquities, who heals all your diseases." The affections of the psalmists are moved toward the God they love and desire, and this is evidence of the work of sanctification which changed their hostility for God into praise. Grudem writes, "God created us not only to glorify him but also to enjoy him and delight in his excellence."[41]

---

[39] Tony Reinke, "The Beauty of Holiness and the Miracle of Sanctification," *Desiring God*, August 24, 2012 (Accessed January 11, 2020), https://www.desiringgod.org/articles/the-beauty-of-holiness-and-the-miracle-of-sanctification.

[40] John Flavel, *The Essential Works of John Flavel* (Louisville, KY: GLH Publishing, 2012), 85.

[41] Grudem, *Systematic Theology*, 1005.

Increased Degree of Praise

The intended result, then, of salvation is to delight in and glorify God. This is what the Apostle Paul is proclaiming in Ephesians 1:3–6. The apostle writes, "to the praise of the glory of His grace, which he freely bestowed on us in the Beloved." Paul awakens the affections of the saints toward God, reminding them of God's gracious election of them in Christ. Bryan Chapell writes, "Predestination is the heavenly Father's shout of eternal love that echoes in our songs of thankful praise as our strength is renewed by the assurance of His care. When predestination is properly taught, it accomplishes what Paul says in His goal: praise to God for His glorious grace and peace to His people."[42] Due to this reality, this writer posits that the Reformed view of election results in greater praise to God. It can be agreed upon that salvation, even generally understood, results in affection for God. However, it is my contention that the greater the understanding that Christians have of God and His work in salvation, the greater the praise and love they will have for him.

The issue can be reduced to the degree of appreciation of salvation. If one espouses the view that God foresaw their exercising of faith and elected them on that basis, then he can have reason to take partial credit for his salvation. If one believes that God predestined the blessings of salvation and not individuals, then the implication is that the overall decision to come to Christ was left to the sinner. He can retain some credit for choosing to be part of the church that receives those predestined benefits. While those in either of these groups are able to praise God for His mercy, grace, and love, they have not delved further into their knowledge of God to truly understand the reality of man's depravity, Christ's work of redemption, the Spirit's work in regeneration, and God's sovereignty in election. For if they did, they would understand their inability to ever come to Christ because of the spiritual darkness of the natural man. They would understand that their ability to believe upon Christ was the gra-

---

[42] Chapell, *Ephesians*, REC, 29.

cious work of God to change their affections. They would understand that God elected individuals, who were not holy and blameless, unto salvation because of His choice to make them the objects of His eternal love. And, they would understand that Christ's death was a real death for sin to truly satisfy their sins before a holy God. When the knowledge of the Christian deepens to understand that salvation is a work of God and God alone, then the already present affections are amplified significantly resulting in greater praise to the Lord.

Questions for Reflection

1. How has your praise and thankfulness been deepened by the biblical doctrine of election?
2. Do you consider the doctrine of election to be a blessing granted by the Lord?
3. Does you view election as being conditional or unconditional? How does your view line up with the Apostle Paul's view?
4. Do you agree that man, in his natural state, requires the intervening work of God?
5. Do you agree that the doctrine of election magnifies God's majesty and glory in the hearts of believers?

Chapter Eight
Strength in Suffering

"The doctrine of God's sovereignty strengthened the martyrs."[1]

The epistle to the Philippians is the joy-producing letter written by the Apostle Paul. He writes to the church at Philippi to encourage them to rejoice in the Lord during their time of suffering and distress. The apostle addresses their difficulties with persecution, and disunity, and provides them with instructions on the Christian life. Williams Hendriksen writes that Paul's purpose of writing to the Philippian church was to give written expression of his gratitude, to provide spiritual guidance, to fill the minds and hearts of the Philippians with the spirit of gladness, and to prevail upon the church to extend Spirit-wrought goodness of heart to Epaphroditus.[2] It is in the first chapter of this epistle that the people of God are encouraged by their sovereign election in Christ, which is demonstrated by the gift of faith, as well as the gift of suffering for the sake of Christ.

The Endurance of the Philippians

The apostle opens the epistle to the Philippians with his common greeting and then writes that he gives thanks to the Lord for their participation in the gospel. Paul writes, "I thank my God in all my remembrance of you, always offering prayer with joy in my every prayer for you all, in view of your participation in the

---

[1] Joel R. Beeke, "Revelation and God," in *Reformed Systematic Theology*, vol. 1, eds. Joel R. Beeke and Paul M. Smalley (Wheaton: Crossway, 2019), 769.

[2] William Hendriksen, *Philippians*, NTC (Grand Rapids: Baker Academic, 2007), 19–21.

gospel from the first day until now" (Phil 1:3–5). The word translated "participation" is the word "fellowship" (*koinonia*). *Koinonia* means "fellowship, partnership, participation, or communion."[3] Hendriksen writes that the meaning of this word in this passage should be understood as a fellowship in warfare: meaning, believers struggle side-by-side against a common foe.[4] John MacArthur echoes this view and states, "When a believer is truly separated from the world, he will come under attack from the world."[5] The Lord warned of such struggles when he said in John 15:19, "If you were of the world, the world would love its own; but because you are not of the world, but I chose you out of the world, because of this the world hates you."

The apostle gives thanks to the Lord for the continued fellowship of warfare the Philippians had with him as they were partakers with him in the defense and confirmation of the gospel (1:7). Paul says that this participation had been "from the first day until now" (v. 5). In other words, their struggle for the sake of the gospel had been occurring since the beginning of their conversion (Acts 16:11–40) until this present time of Paul's writing. J. A. Motyer writes that the apostle saw in the Philippians perseverance, endurance, and identification with the gospel wherever it was called into question as they jumped to its defense.[6] Motyer goes on to state, "Their association with the gospel was not transient, nor conditional upon favorable circumstances. Nor was it silent. They kept on in their faith; they held on to their faith in opposition; they spoke up when their faith was challenged."[7] In other words, the genuineness of the Philippians' faith was well attested by their willingness to endure hardship for the sake of the gospel. According to the teaching of the Lord Jesus in the Parable of the Sower (Matt 13:1–23), the faith of the Philippians was

---

[3] Mounce, *Analytical Lexicon to the Greek New Testament*, 286.

[4] Hendriksen, *Philippians*, NTC, 52.

[5] John MacArthur, *Philippians*, MacNTC (Chicago: Moody, 2001), 25.

[6] J. A. Motyer, *The Message of the Philippians*, BST (Downers Grove: InterVarsity Press, 1984), 47.

[7] Motyer, *Message of the Philippians*, BST, 47.

not shallow, or divided between the world and Christ. Their faith was deeply rooted in the gospel.

He Who Began a Good Work

Paul's joy in their perseverance was founded in the reality of God's work in them as he states, "He who had begun a good work in you will perfect it until the day of Christ Jesus" (1:6). This is the foundational truth that gives the Philippians strength during their distress. Here, the apostle's confidence is grounded in the Lord's sovereign work in their lives. Dennis Johnson writes:

> Paul knows full well—and the Philippians must remember it, too—that the only reason that they have been his partners in the gospel from the first day to the present is that God began a good work in them, and that God has sustained that work and is sustaining that work today. Because the sovereign work of the invincible God is the source of the Philippians' faith, Paul can be confident that God, the Master Builder, will carry on his construction project until he has finished the job.[8]

Motyer adds that Paul had confidence in the Philippians because he viewed them as a work of God. Motyer writes, "In verse 3, he thanks God when he thinks of them. In verse 6, he views them as begun, continued, and completed by divine workmanship."[9] From beginning to end, Paul's confidence is grounded in God's work in their lives. Steve Lawson states, "If God has caused you to be born again, you can be assured that he will complete this

---

[8] Dennis Johnson, *Philippians*, REC (Philipsburg, NJ: P&R Publishing, 2013), 31.

[9] Motyer, *Message of Philippians*, BST, 48. He writes, "Really, therefore, Paul's confidence for the Philippians arose from the fact that he saw them as a work of God. In verse 3, he thanks God when he thinks of them. If there is anything worthy of praise among them, God is its Author. In verse 6, he views them as begun, continued, and completed by divine workmanship. In verse 7, their lives bear fruit because they partake of God's grace. God is at work, and where God works he will certainly accomplish the task."

work 'until the day of Christ Jesus.' As a believer in Christ, you are as certain of heaven as though you have already been there ten thousand years. God finishes what he starts."[10]

The emphasis on God's work in regeneration is a clear indication that God, not any man, has begun this work in the heart, and he will complete His work of salvation through the process of sanctification. This reality provides strength to the one enduring various trials, because the same God who actively brought the person to faith is the same God who is actively working in the life of the sufferer to bring about holiness in his life. Consider God's direct work in regeneration. Regeneration is the "act of God awakening spiritual life within us, bringing us from spiritual death to spiritual life."[11] This aspect of salvation demonstrates the intimate involvement of God in the beginning of the salvation of His elect. God sovereignly causes His people to be born again, or else, none would come to him. John 1:12–13 states, "But as many as received him, to them he gave the right to become children of God, even to those who believe in His name, who were born, not of blood nor of the will of the flesh nor of the will of man, but of God." Andreas Köstenberger writes the following:

> Some identify "children of God," not "those who believe," as the antecedent of the relative clause beginning 1:13 in order not to make faith follow regeneration. However, this is both syntactically awkward and implausible, as well as theologically unnecessary. In the Greek syntax, "those who believe" immediately precedes the relative clause and is thus most naturally taken as the antecedent, and the relationship between faith and rebirth is not easily reduced to a set sequential formula. The statement in 1 John 5:1, "Everyone who believes that Jesus is the Christ is born of God," allows one to deduce from a person's belief that person's regenerate state; regeneration and saving faith thus go together and cannot be

---

[10] Steve Lawson, *Philippians for You* (Charlotte: The Good Book Company, 2017), 33.

[11] Grudem, *Systematic Theology*, 702.

separated. Spiritual rebirth takes place at God's initiative; people are called to faith based on God's revelation in Christ.[12]

D. A. Carson writes, "It is true that no one is born from God who does not receive Christ and believe on his name; but it is equally true that no one receives Christ and believes on his name, who is not born of God."[13]

In addition, John 3:3-8 is another passage that places being born of the Spirit before entering or seeing the kingdom of God which takes place at conversion. The reference to the kingdom could be in view of the full manifestation of the kingdom yet to be fulfilled at the consummation of all things, or the reality of the sinner's entrance into the present, spiritual kingdom at conversion. Jesus says, "Truly, truly, I say to you, unless one is born again he cannot see the kingdom of God" (v. 3), and, "Truly, truly, I say to you, unless one is born of water and the Spirit he cannot enter into the kingdom of God" (v. 5). John Murray states,

Whether we think of being begotten of the Spirit or of being born of the Spirit, one thing is certain—we are instructed by our Lord that for entrance into the kingdom of God we are wholly dependent upon the action of the Holy Spirit, an action of the Holy Spirit which is compared to that action on the part of our parents by which we were born into the world. We are as dependent upon the Holy Spirit as we are upon the action of our parents in connection with our natural birth. We were not begotten by our father because we decided to be. We were simply begotten and we were born. . . . We do not have spiritual perception of the Kingdom of God, nor do we enter into it because we willed to or decided to. If this privilege is ours, it is because the Holy Spirit willed it

---

[12] Andreas J. Köstenberger, *John*, BECNT (Grand Rapids: Baker Academic, 2004), 39.

[13] D. A. Carson, *Divine Sovereignty and Human Responsibility: Biblical Perspective in Tension* (Eugene, OR: Wipf and Stock Publishers, 2002), 182.

and here all rests upon the Holy Spirit's decision and action. He begets or bears when and where he pleases.[14]

MacArthur and Mayhue write, "Into darkened and dead hearts he speaks the command, 'Let there be light,' and instantaneously births in us the light of eternal spiritual life where it had not existed."[15]

The parallel passage of John 3:5 is Ezekiel 36:25–27, where salvation is described as a cleansing that God alone performs on the sinner. Köstenberger describes it as follows:

"Born again/from above" in 3:3 [of John] is further explained as "born of water and spirit" in 3:5. Rather than referring to water and spirit baptism, two kinds of birth, or a variety of other things, the phrase probably denotes one spiritual birth. This is suggested by the fact that "born again/from above in 3:3, by the use of one preposition (*ex*) to govern both phrases in 3:5, and by the antecedent OT (prophetic) theology. The closest OT parallel is Ezek. 36:25–27, which presages God's cleansing of human hearts with water and their inner transformation by his Spirit.[16]

It is important to see that all of the singular, first-person pronouns in this passage refer to God. He says, "I will sprinkle clean water on you [meaning the purifying work of the Spirit], I will take out your heart of stone and give you a heart of flesh [regeneration], and I will put My Spirit in you [regeneration]" (Ezek 36:25–27). This is a work of God and God alone from start to finish in which he actively brings the spiritually dead sinner to life and makes him a new creation. MacArthur and Mayhue state, "In regeneration, man is entirely passive; God is the sole active agent in bringing about the creative miracle of the new birth."[17]

---

[14] John Murray, *Redemption Accomplished and Applied*, (Grand Rapids: William B. Eerdmans Publishing, 2015), 103.

[15] MacArthur and Mayhue, *Biblical Doctrine*, 580.

[16] Köstenberger, *John*, BECNT, 124.

[17] Köstenberger, *John*, BECNT, 577.

Regeneration demonstrates the intimate involvement of God in the initiation of salvation. This is Paul's point in Philippians 1:6 that "He who began a good work in you will perfect it until the day of Christ Jesus." The work of God in the beginnings of salvation continues throughout even the most difficult circumstances in life, specifically, the trials and suffering the Philippians endured as a result of their faith in Christ. God is sovereignly and intimately involved in every aspect of the Christian's life. It is also necessary to point out that God is not simply responding to the plight of His people by encouraging them, but has actively ordained that His people endure this ordeal for the purpose of growing in their faith.

God's Gift of Suffering

In Philippians 1:27–30, the apostle reiterates God's initial work in salvation with granting them faith, but also His sovereign work of granting them the privilege of suffering for the sake of Christ. This gift is also a grace of God. The English phrase, "has been granted," translates the Greek verb *charizō*, which is from the same root word as the noun *charis* ("grace") and literally means "to grant graciously."[18] It is a gift of divine grace that the Philippian church was privileged to suffer for the sake of Christ. Of this blessing of suffering for Christ, Hendriksen writes, "It brings Christ nearer to the soul of the Christian, it brings assurance of salvation, the conviction that the Spirit of glory and the Spirit of God rests upon the sufferer, it will be rewarded in the hereafter, it is a means of winning unbelievers, and it leads to the frustration of Satan and the glorification of God."[19] Hendriksen adds that in suffering, the Christian begins to understand the Christ who suffered for him and receives the sweet enduring fellowship with him. Job himself stated with regards to his own suffering in Job 42:5, "I have heard of You by the hearing of the ear;

---

[18] MacArthur, *Philippians*, MacNTC, 95.

[19] Hendriksen, *Philippians*, NTC, 90–91.

but now my eye sees you." In other words, suffering and tribulation brings the Christian into a more intimate relationship and dependence upon the Lord, and this the Lord is actively performing in their lives.

The apostle's words to the Philippians brings them to the realization of the grace of God in their struggles and the fortitude of mind that he provides to them. John Calvin writes, "At that time the most cruel persecutions raged almost everywhere, because Satan strove with all his might to impede the commencement of the gospel, and was the more enraged in proportion as Christ put forth powerfully the grace of His Spirit."[20] Not only was suffering granted to them, but also the strength to withstand the trials. The apostle states, "In no way alarmed by your opponents—which is a sign of destruction for them, but of salvation for you, and that too, from God" (Phil 1:28). The courage provided to the Philippians is a clear indication of God's work in them. Hendriksen writes,

> The reason why this undaunted courage is proof of salvation and of invincibility is that it is not man-made. Hence, Paul adds, 'and this from God' . . . such fearlessness can and must be considered a gift of God, the product of His Spirit working in the heart, then certainly the conclusion follows that he who began a good work will carry it on toward completion."[21]

Paul states that he experiences the same conflicts; this too, would have been a source of strength for the church—if Christ's apostle experiences suffering, and this for the sake of the gospel, then their suffering, also, is for the furtherance of the gospel.

Big God Theology

Suffering and trials are acknowledged to be part of the Christian life by both Reformed and Arminian Christians. However,

---

[20] John Calvin, *Philippians*, CC (Grand Rapids: Baker Books, 2009), 49.

[21] Hendriksen, *Philippians*, NTC, 89–90.

the fundamental difference between the two is whether or not God allows the freewill, evil actions of men to bring about good, or if God has decreed the evil actions of men for the good of His will. Reformed believers confess that the suffering experienced in this life is decreed by God, and does not occur by chance. Derek Thomas writes:

> God weaves, not only the fabric that produces joy and right-eousness, but also that which produces agony and evil. Both strands in the tapestry eventually will lead us to glorify God even if we don't quite understand how or why he sometimes chooses a path that involves so much pain.[22]

In other words, Thomas teaches that pain and suffering are sovereignly ordained by God to lead His people to glory in him. In contrast to this view, Walls and Dongell give another view of God's active/inactive role in suffering, and provide a hypothetical situation of a teenager who becomes paralyzed after an automobile accident caused by the failure of his brakes. They write,

> We believe that a brake failure and the resulting crash that causes paralysis need not be understood as sent by God. Rather, the brake failure can be seen as a tragedy resulting from the fact that we live in a world operating by God–ordained natural law and that sometimes things designed by human beings fail. In this world, where God "sends rain on the righteous and the unrighteous" (Matt 5:45), all of us are recipients of good gifts from God's natural order even as we are vulnerable to the suffering it can cause. Gravity, like rain, is a good thing, but sometimes both of these contribute to tragic accidents. This is what is essentially involved in living as embodied beings in a physical world.[23]

According to Walls and Dongell, the only involvement God had in the car wreck scenario was that he has fixed a natural law in

---

[22] Derek Thomas, "A Pastoral Theology of Suffering," *Reformed Faith and Practice* vol. 1, no. 3 (December 2016): 74.

[23] Walls and Dongell, *Why I Am Not a Calvinist*, 209.

the world where sometimes bad things happen. It is not His fault, but rather tragedies occur as part of living in this fallen physical world. Whereas Thomas acknowledges God's direct involvement in suffering, Walls and Dongell dismiss that claim and relegate suffering as simply being part of life. However, the Apostle Paul's words appear to conflict with Walls and Dongell.

The words of the Apostle Paul in Philippians 1:29 present God as being ultimately responsible for the suffering of the Philippians. Again, Paul's words to them are, "For to you it has been granted for Christ's sake, not only to believe in him, but also to suffer for His sake." Silva states the following:

> Paul's description of suffering as a gift, *hymin echaristhe*, is lexically unique in the NT. It is also startling. Believers find it difficult enough to accept the inevitability of suffering; we feel we are making spiritual progress if we resign ourselves to the fact that grief cannot be avoided. But here the apostle challenges the Philippians' theology and asks them to understand their afflictions not merely as inevitable but as a manifestation of God's gracious dealings with them.[24]

Joseph Hellerman states, "God had graciously given to the Philippians the privilege of continuing to believe in his Son even while suffering and undergoing persecution."[25] He further states, "The strong emphasis on divine sovereignty—regarding both faith and suffering—should not be missed."[26] The phrase, *to huper autou paschein*, which means, "to suffer for His sake" refers to, "a privilege, a special grace which surpasses even the grace of being able to believe in Christ."[27] This gift of suffering was not a matter of God simply creating natural laws and working good out of

---

[24] Moisés Silva, *Philippians*, BECNT, 2nd ed. (Grand Rapids: Baker Academic, 2005), 125.

[25] Joseph Hellermen, *Philippians*, EGGNT (Nashville: B&H Publishing, 2015), 134.

[26] Hellermen, *Philippians*, EGGNT, 134.

[27] Hellermen, *Philippians*, EGGNT, 134.

them when bad things happen. Rather, God had directly privileged the Philippians to suffer for Christ's sake. The implication, then, is that God ordained their suffering for His glory rather than God simply had "foreknowledge" that they would suffer at the hands of evil men and decided to allow it. The text describes an active role of God decreeing their circumstance, providing for them in their circumstance, growing their faith in their circumstance, and glorifying himself in their circumstance.

As Walls and Dongell demonstrated, the Arminians will not see suffering as that which God brings about in the lives of His people. This view conflicts with Paul's words that God granted this to the Philippians, which implies that God was not idle, but actively and sovereignly the Initiator. Geisler, however, writes that the suffering of the Philippians "was not something God did for them. Both [faith and suffering] were simply an opportunity God gave them to use 'on the behalf of Christ' by their free choice."[28] By contrast, the Scripture states in Lamentations 3:37–38, "Who is there who speaks and it comes to pass, unless the Lord has commanded it? Is it not from the mouth of the Most High that both good and ill go forth?" Job states in Job 1:21, "Naked I came from my mother's womb, and naked I shall return there. The Lord gave and the Lord has taken away. Blessed be the name of the Lord." Job also stated to his wife, "Shall we indeed accept good from God and not accept adversity?" (Job 2:10). Thomas Watson writes,

> God does not bring His people into troubles, and leave them there. He will stand by them; he will hold their heads and hearts when they are fainting. And there is another promise, "He is their strength in the time of trouble" (Ps 37:39). "Oh," says the soul, "I shall faint in the day of trial." But God will be the strength of our hearts; he will join His forces with us. Either he will make His hand lighter, or our faith stronger.[29]

---

[28] Geisler, *Chosen but Free*, 189.

[29] Thomas Watson, *All Things for Good* (Carlisle, PA: Banner of Truth, 2011), 16.

Watson also states, "Whoever brings an affliction to us, it is God that sends it."[30] The Lord is not passive in suffering. He brings about the sanctification of His people through times of suffering, as he did with the Philippians.

The same God who began a good work and granted to them faith, is the same God who actively continues working in their lives through their suffering to accomplish His sanctifying work. This is true of all believers, Beloved. The time of suffering and trials are not simply natural law, for where then is the comfort for the saints? If something can happen to God's people that he is not in control of or directly involved in, then how can believers be encouraged to know that God is using this for their good? When believers recognize that the same God who loved them from beginning and chose them from foundation of the world appoints trials, then they can confidently be assured and thereby strengthened, that the sovereign God is bringing about what is good and right according to His will. Again, as Watson states, "Out of the most poisonous drugs God extracts our salvation. . . . No vessel can be made of gold without fire; so it is impossible that we should be made vessels of honor, unless we are melted and refined in the furnace of affliction."[31]

Questions for Reflection

1. What struggles have you endured? Has the knowledge of God's sovereignty strengthened you?
2. Is your confidence of having eternal life grounded in God's choosing of you or of you choosing him?
3. Do you reflect on God's active role in the midst of suffering and trials? Does this encourage you to persevere?
4. Do you agree that regeneration precedes faith? How does your view line up with the biblical teaching?
5. Do you agree that God has decreed all things, good and bad, for His glory? How does this affect your outlook in the midst of pain?

---

[30] Watson, *All Things for Good*, 25.
[31] Watson, *All Things for Good*, 26.

Chapter Nine
A Weapon Against Pride

"God elects us in order to eliminate all boasting, all self-reliance, all human pride."[1]

Another result of understanding the doctrine of election correctly is that of humility. The epistle of James states, "God is opposed to the proud, but gives grace to the humble" (Jas 4:6). This truth is expressed in numerous places in Scripture (e.g. Rom 12:16; Eph 4:2; Phil 2:3; Jas 4:10; 1 Pet 5:6). The question is, if God commands us to be humble, then how do we cultivate humility in our lives? What is the catalyst that brings us to the point of humility rather than walking in pride? The answer goes back to the truth of God's sovereign election of sinners. In 1 Corinthians 1:26-31, the Apostle Paul decimates the possibility of pride among Christians with the reminder of God's sovereign and unconditional call upon their lives.

Setting of 1 Corinthians

The Corinthian church was divided by factions. The apostle addresses their disunity from the very beginning of his letter: "Now I exhort you, brethren, by the name of our Lord Jesus Christ, that you all agree and that there be no divisions among you, but that you be made complete in the same mind and in the same judgment. For I have been informed concerning you, my brethren, by Chloe's people, that there are quarrels among you" (1:10-11). From the outset of the letter, the apostle addresses this

---

[1] G. K. Beale, *1 and 2 Thessalonians* (Downers Grove: InterVarsity Press, 2003), 228.

topic of church unity as of first importance. John MacArthur writes, "Among the Corinthian church's many sins and short-comings, quarreling is the one that Paul chose to deal with first."[2] Factions had developed among the church members and their favorite ministers. Thomas Schreiner states, "The Christians were picking sides and choosing different ministers. Some sided with Paul, others with Apollos, and still others with Peter."[3] It was characteristic of the culture in that day to align with a particular philosopher over another, and this practice was occurring in the church of Jesus Christ. MacArthur states that the Corinthians had trusted in Christ for their redemption, but because of their love for human wisdom, they desired to add the wisdom of their culture to their Christianity, which then produced these factions.[4] The result of these factions was pride and self-centeredness.

The Effectual Calling of God

As a result of the factions and worldly wisdom that was adopted by the church, the Apostle Paul begins to expound what true wisdom really is. Paul brings the glorious gospel of Christ to the forefront of the discussion, and contrasts God's wisdom with that of the world's wisdom. Schreiner writes, "Paul explains why the message of the cross is foolishness to unbelievers, but the saved realize that the cross unleashes God's transforming power. Paul emphasizes God's sovereignty, and, with a quote from

---

[2] John MacArthur, *1 Corinthians*, MacNTC (Chicago: Moody Publishers, 1984), 25.

[3] Thomas Schreiner, *1 Corinthians*, TNTC (Downers Grove: IVP Academic, 2018), 62.

[4] MacArthur, *1 Corinthians*, MacNTC, 36. He writes, "Unfortunately many of the Corinthian converts carried their spirit of philosophical factionalism into the church. Some of them still held onto beliefs of their former pagan philosophy. They were divided not only regarding Christian leaders (1:12) but also regarding philosophical viewpoints. They would not get over their love for human wisdom. They had trusted in Christ and recognized their redemption by grace through the cross, but they wanted to add human wisdom to what He had done for them."

Isaiah 29:14, stresses that God rejects the wisdom of the world."[5] The apostle states in verse 24, "but to those who are the called, both Jews and Greeks, Christ the power of God and wisdom of God." It is in this verse that we see a hint of a truth that will be explained further in verses 26–31, that this calling is effectual to all who receive it.

The calling that is referred to in this text by the Apostle Paul is the effectual calling of God. Charles Hodge writes that "the called" always means those who are effectually called of God. He states, "There is a twofold call of the gospel: the one external by the word; the other internal by the Spirit. The subjects of the latter are designated 'the called.'"[6] This effectual calling of God harkens back to the previous truth discussed of the new birth. It is a divine work of God in the heart of the sinner. The effectual calling and regeneration, though distinct, occur simultaneously. John MacArthur and Richard Mayhue state of the effectual calling, "He [God] powerfully summons the sinner out of his spiritual death and blindness and, by virtue of the creative power of his word, imparts new life to him—giving him a new heart, along with eyes to see and ears to hear, and thus enabling him to repent and believe in Christ for salvation."[7] The effectual calling of God achieves its desired effect; he calls, and those whom he calls respond in faith and repentance because of their new birth by the Holy Spirit.

---

[5] Schreiner, *1 Corinthians*, TNTC, 66.

[6] Charles Hodge, *A Commentary on I & II Corinthians* (Carlisle, PA: Banner of Truth, 1978), 23.

[7] MacArthur and Mayhue, *Biblical Doctrine*, 577. This is also echoed by R. C. Sproul: "The effectual call of God is an inward call. It is the secret work of quickening or regeneration accomplished in the souls of the elect by the immediate supernatural operation of the Holy Spirit. It effects or works the inward change of the disposition, inclination, and desire for the soul" (*Essential Truths of the Christian Faith*, 177).

The Fallen Nature of Man

It is extremely important to understand the effectual calling of God because none would ever come to Christ apart from it. The Scripture teaches that unregenerate man is morally corrupt. When Adam and Eve sinned and rebelled against the Lord (Gen 3), the image of God in which they were created was marred, and as a result, their descendants are now in bondage to sin. The Fall affected man to his very core, and he is now inclined to wickedness. Consider these Scriptures describing man's spiritual condition:

> Then the Lord saw that the wickedness of man was great on the earth, and that every intent of the thoughts of his heart was only evil continually (Gen 6:5).

> The Lord smelled the soothing aroma; and the Lord said to himself, "I will never again curse the ground on account of man, for the intent of man's heart is evil from his youth; and I will never again destroy every living thing, as I have done" (Gen 8:21).

> The heart is more deceitful than all else and is desperately sick; who can understand it? (Jer 17:9).

> As it is written, "There is none righteous, not even one; there is none who understands, there is none who seeks for God; all have turned aside, together they have become useless; there is none who does good, there is not even one" (Rom 3:10–12).

> And you were dead in your trespasses and sins, in which you formerly walked according to the course of this world, according to the prince of the power of the air, of the spirit that is now working in the sons of disobedience. Among them we too all formerly lived in the lusts of our flesh, indulging the desires of the flesh and of the mind, and were by nature children of wrath, even as the rest. But God, being rich in mercy, because of His great love with which he loved us, (Eph 2:1–4).

The Scriptures teach that there is nothing good in man. Mankind is in a fallen state and is under the wrath of God. All are in rebellion against a holy God, for all are in a state of total depravity. Duane Spencer states, "Total Depravity means that man in his natural state is incapable of doing anything or desiring anything pleasing to God."[8] Furthermore, Sproul helpfully explains that total depravity does not mean that man is as evil as he could be, but rather the Fall affected man's mind, will, and body. Man is radically corrupted.[9]

John Gerstner states, "The natural man hates God, hates his fellow man, and hates himself. He would kill God if he could, does kill man when he can, and commits spiritual suicide every day. We are the dirty soil in which God plants His flower, and from our filth, produces a thing of divine beauty."[10] Man is at enmity with God, and left to himself, he will never come in peace to his great enemy.

Why is man not able to come to God? As stated previously, man's will is fallen. Man is bound by his very nature, which is only sinful; therefore, to choose Christ is contrary to his very nature. Jonathan Edwards states concerning the will of man: "And therefore I observe, that the will is plainly, that by which the mind chooses anything. The faculty of the will is that faculty or power of principle of mind by which it is capable of choosing; an act of the will is the same as an act of choosing or choice."[11] It is

---

[8] Duane E. Spencer, *TULIP: The Five Points of Calvinism in Light of Scripture* (Grand Rapids: Baker Books, 1979), 33.

[9] Sproul, *Essential Truths of the Christian Faith*, 153. He writes, "Total depravity means radical corruption. We must be careful to note the difference between total depravity and utter depravity. To be utterly depraved is to be as wicked as one could possibly be. Hitler was extremely depraved, but he could have been worse than he was. I am a sinner. Yet I could sin more often and more severely than I actually do. I am not utterly depraved, but I am totally depraved. For total depravity means that I and everyone else are depraved or corrupt in the totality of our being. There is no part of us that is left untouched by sin. Our minds, our wills, and our bodies are affected by evil."

[10] John Gerstner, "The Atonement and the Purpose of God," in Gabriel N. E. Fluhrer, ed. *Atonement* (Philipsburg, NJ: P&R Publishing, 2010), 50.

[11] Jonathan Edwards, *Freedom of the Will* (New Haven, CT: Yale University Press, 2009), 137.

the will that chooses to do something or not. Choosing Christ or the things of God having only a fallen will is an act which is contrary to its very desires. The unbelieving heart does not desire God, and therefore would not choose God. It is for this reason that the effectual calling of God is needed, so that through the regenerating work of the Spirit and the granting of faith, the sinner may believe upon Christ and repent.

A Lowly Calling

Having expounded the nature and necessity of the effectual calling of God, we are then able to understand clearly the force of the Apostle Paul's reminder to the Corinthians of their low estate and dependence upon the Lord for their salvation. The apostle states, "For consider your calling brethren, that there were not many wise according to the flesh. Not many mighty, not many noble" (1:26). Paul uses the words *sophoi* (wise), *dunatoi* (powerful men), and *eugeneis* (well-born) with the negative *ou* (not) to describe the social standing of the believing Corinthians. They had no reason to boast before anyone, and this is the apostle's point. Paul is summoning the Corinthians to "behold" their calling. *Blepete* (behold) is a command by the apostle and has the meaning of "discern mentally," or, "perceive."[12] Paul basically says, "give careful, deep thought to God's call to you." Richard Pratt states the following:

> The Corinthians needed to remember something about their status in the world when they were called. When they had first received the gospel, most of them were not wise by human standards. They were neither influential nor of noble birth. When they were called, they had no basis from which to assert superiority over one another or to boast because they had no wisdom, no status, and no power. Yet, when God called them, they believed the simple gospel. Unfortunately, many of the Corinthians had

---

[12] Mounce, *Analytical Lexicon to the Greek New Testament*, 118.

forgotten this experience and had appealed to human wisdom to exalt themselves and to divide from one another.[13]

Pride built up in their hearts; however, the Apostle Paul's reminder of their calling was a weapon against their pride, for their salvation was not dependent upon their wisdom, but upon God who brought it about.

Paul's description of their low social standing was not intended to belittle them, but to bring them back to the awareness of God's mercy toward them. Lawson writes,

> According to His perfect wisdom, God has chosen not to call many whom the world would consider to be wise, mighty, or noble. Instead, for the most part, God has called the very opposite—the foolish, weak, and ignoble. He chooses to call to himself those who are viewed as nothing by the world. By this inverted standard, God alone receives credit for the salvation of His people.[14]

Charles Hodge states that the words used by the apostle are meant to signify to the church that in general they were not from the higher ranks of society: not many great in the sense of power and authority, and not many noble or well-born.[15]

Paul goes on to state, "But God has chosen the foolish things of the world to shame the wise, and God has chosen the weak things of the world to shame the things which are strong" (1:27). The apostle leaves no stone unturned with his words in order to cut directly through the pride of the Corinthians. The Greek word *mōra* means, "dull, foolish,"[16] and *asthenā* is defined as "deficient in authority, dignity, or power."[17] Schreiner states,

---

[13] Richard Pratt, *I & II Corinthians*, HNTC (Nashville: B&H Publishing, 2000), 23.

[14] Lawson, *Foundations of Grace*, 391.

[15] Hodge, *I & II Corinthians*, 24.

[16] Mounce, *Analytical Lexicon to the Greek New Testament*, 325.

[17] Mounce, *Analytical Lexicon to the Greek New Testament*, 102.

Just as the cross reverses human expectations in terms of how the world will be saved, so too, God chose to save the most unlikely candidates—the foolish and weak. Those who are not esteemed for their wisdom and those who lack political power are among those whom God has savingly called to himself. . . . They are "the nothings" (*ta mē onta*) of the world. Two ironies surface here. First, the Corinthians desired to be people of status and respect, but God most often chooses those who do not possess such qualities. Second, even though they took pride in such status, they actually lacked it themselves. In other words, their grasping after such an honor revealed their own insecurities.[18]

The apostle crushes the social standing values of the culture that the Corinthians allowed to influence them. As Paul points out, they are the foolish and the weak, and he goes on to state they are "the despised" (v. 28). MacArthur points out Paul's use of the Greek perfect tense with the word "despised" in verse 28. He writes that this indicates that what was once despised among men will continue to be despised, "so people who were thought to be nobodies in society would continue to be thought of as nobodies."[19] This is indeed a powerful means to knock someone off the proverbial "high horse."

The Corinthians needed to be reminded that it was God's grace alone that brought about their salvation. Richard Pratt states that the wise and powerful indeed tend to boast of becoming Christians as if they deserved it or by their own wisdom have found it. In their eyes they become the elite because of their sophistication. Paul's purpose was to bring them to the understanding that they had nothing in and of themselves to boast about regarding their salvation. Pratt adds, "To dispel any pride remaining in the Corinthians, Paul reminded them why they believed the gospel. It was not because they were wise or powerful

---

[18] Schreiner, *1 Corinthians*, TNTC, 72–73.

[19] MacArthur, *1 Corinthians*, MacNTC, 51.

enough to receive salvation. It was because of God that they were in Christ Jesus."[20]

God's Action

Paul's rebuke culminates in his words, "But by His doing you are in Christ Jesus, who became to us wisdom from God, and righteousness and sanctification and redemption, so that, just as it is written, 'Let him who boasts, boast in the Lord'" (1:30–31). If there was any question of what Paul was trying to say, it was made clear in these verses. Their salvation was "by His doing" or more literally, "from him" you are in Christ Jesus.[21] This was a work of God and a work of God alone. It was Christ, the true wisdom, who became to them wisdom [the insight into the true nature of things[22]] from God. Schreiner writes, "Wisdom . . . does not centre on rhetorical brilliance, but has a soteriological character, which reminds readers of their greatest need."[23] Being united to Christ Jesus grants to the believers a wisdom that makes them truly wise, and "the following terms, *righteousness*, *holiness*, and *redemption*, unpack the nature of true wisdom."[24] Schreiner adds,

---

[20] Pratt, *I & II Corinthians*, HNTC, 24. He writes, "The wise, powerful, and sophisticated of the world tend to boast that they become Christians because they deserve to be the people of God. The elect become the elite in their own minds. In the same way, the Corinthians boast of being 'of Paul' or 'of Apollos'—the source of the divisions in the church—demonstrated forgetfulness that their salvation never depended upon their own merit. But the lowly of the earth understand that they have nothing in themselves of which to boast. They know they do not deserve to be in Christ's kingdom. Therefore, God chooses these kinds of people so that no one may boast before him."

[21] Schreiner, *1 Corinthians*, TNTC, 74.

[22] W. E. Vine, Merrill Unger, and William White Jr., *Vine's Complete Expository Dictionary of Old and New Testament Words* (Nashville: Thomas Nelson, 1996), 3020.

[23] Schreiner, *1 Corinthians*, TNTC, 74.

[24] Schreiner, *1 Corinthians*, TNTC, 74.

Righteousness designates the gift of righteousness, of right standing with God so that believers are not condemned by God. . . . The next term, holiness, often translated "sanctification," is also significant soteriologically. The word is often used of progress in holiness, but it does not have that import here. In this context, the word designates positional or definitive sanctification: the holiness that belongs to all believers by virtue of their union with Christ. Paul first speaks of the legal sphere—believers stand in the right before God. Then he shifts to the cultic sphere—believers are clean and holy before God. The last term to describe wisdom is redemption. . . . The redemption of which Paul speaks (and so also the righteousness and holiness) is rooted in the cross of Christ by which we are secured. Once again Paul emphasizes that wisdom resides not in talk but in power.[25]

The apostle's point, then, is that because of God and God alone, the Corinthians are in Christ. The wisdom they sought previously came as result of God's effectual calling, and by faith, the wisdom of God was granted to them. Apart from His calling, they were unrighteous, unholy, weak, and foolish slaves to sin.

No Room for Pride

The biblical doctrine of election, understood rightly, brings the attention of the believer back to the Lord who called him. God's calling was effectual, unconditional, and was His work alone. When reflecting upon the Apostle Paul's words in 1 Corinthians 1:26–31, pride is crushed and brought to naught. What credit of one's salvation can any take unto himself? He has nothing to boast about in himself. As Joel Beeke states,

Rather than promoting pride and elitism, election is a profoundly humbling doctrine for believers. It keeps us from trying to reverse roles with God (Rom 9:6–23). It persuades

---

[25] Schreiner, *1 Corinthians*, TNTC, 74.

us to let God be God by teaching us there are some things that God has not revealed to us because they are not good for us to know. . . . Election also humbles us by making us realize that we owe everything to God's grace. If our eyes have been opened, we see that our salvation is entirely due to the sovereign love and pity of our God, and not to any merit of our own. Election grace initiates our salvation, accomplishes it, and preserves it.[26]

There is nothing at all whereby any can boast before God, but rather they are left to the realization that God is the One who began this good work in them by sheer grace. The Corinthians had no reason to boast before the Lord and neither do any other believers.

The Arminian believers are not incapable of being humble before the Lord, but their humility is not and cannot be to the degree to which the Apostle Paul speaks. Of course, the Arminians put forth the teaching of prevenient grace, but such "grace" is not sufficient to bring sinners to realization of their spiritual state apart from God. Arminian Roger Olsen writes that prevenient grace is "the illuminating, convicting, calling, and enabling power of the Holy Spirit working on the sinner's soul and making them free to choose saving grace (or reject it)."[27] In other words, this grace brings the dead, unregenerate sinner to a state of neutrality, whereby he may choose Christ or reject Christ if he so desires. If one believes in prevenient grace then he has reason to boast before the Lord because when the Holy Spirit brought him to this place of supposed neutrality, even though he is unregenerate, the sinner chose to do the noblest act of existence and believe upon Christ for his salvation. Since the Arminians reject the belief that the new birth is necessary first, they are left with acknowledging that they, out of their own free-will, chose Christ without the regenerating work of the Spirit of God. Partial credit,

---

[26] Joel Beeke, *Living for God's Glory: An Introduction to Calvinism* (Lake Mary, FL: Reformation Trust, 2008), 69.

[27] Olsen, *Against Calvinism*, 67.

then, is due to them, and therefore, their humility before God is not to its intended, potential degree.

In contrast to the Arminian view, Paul's words to the Corinthians squelch that view and establish that God alone is reason that any are in Christ. According to the Apostle Paul, his worldly wisdom was not enough to reveal the glorious gospel because worldly wisdom is foolishness before God. His popularity and greatness among the culture was not sufficient because God primarily calls the despised and weak. He cannot pride himself in his ability to believe the gospel because, as already expounded, by God's doing, the apostle, like the Corinthians, was in Christ. Humility is born out of a realization of how grand, majestic, and merciful the glorious God is toward sinners, and how sinful and hopeless all are without His grace working in their hearts to bring about salvation. The Lord did not simply have a knowledge of who would believe in him, but rather the Lord actively chose whom he would place in Christ. Otherwise, the sinner does have reason to boast. The doctrine of election rightly understood is a weapon against pride and cultivates a greater humility before God.

Questions for Reflection

1. Do you agree that God's effectual calling always achieves its purpose? Do you see the necessity of the effectual calling of God?
2. Do you agree that the Fall affected man to his very core? Mind, will, and affections?
3. How has the biblical view of man's depravity shaped your view of freewill?
4. Do you recognize that God's grace alone has brought about your salvation?
5. Do you see the doctrine of election as a means to cultivate humility in your life?

Chapter Ten
The Foundation of the Christian Character

*"The only pathway by which the elect attain glory is the road of faith
and holiness. The knowledge of God's electing love for us begets in us an
imitating love."*[1]

As demonstrated previously, the biblical doctrine of election
crushes the pride of the believer as he realizes that his salvation
was a total work of God and of God alone. The biblical doctrine of
election is also the foundation for the Christian character we are
to exhibit toward others. The Apostle Paul states in Ephesians
5:1-2, "Therefore be imitators of God, as beloved children; and
walk in love, just as Christ also loved you and gave himself up for
us, an offering and a sacrifice to God as a fragrant aroma." The
qualities now to be expected of God's people are patterned after
Christ our Lord. The Apostle Paul labors this point in Colossians
3:12-14 when he states,

> So, as those who have been chosen of God, holy and beloved,
> put on a heart of compassion, kindness, humility, gentleness
> and patience; bearing with one another, and forgiving each
> other, whoever has a complaint against anyone; just as the
> Lord forgave you, so also should you. Beyond all these things
> put on love, which is the perfect bond of unity.

In the previous context the Apostle Paul expounded to the
Colossians of the reality of their conversion to Christ. They are
new creatures, for he says that they have "put on the new self

---

[1] Joel Beeke, "Revelation and God," *Reformed Systematic Theology*, vol. 1, eds.
Joel R. Beeke and Paul M. Smalley (Wheaton, IL: Crossway, 2019), 1052.

who is being renewed to a true knowledge according to the image of the One who created him" (3:10). John MacArthur states, "Salvation is transformation—the old self is gone, replaced by the new self."[2] MacArthur, then, quotes R. C. H. Lenski, "The old man is not converted, he cannot be; he is not renewed, he cannot be. He can only be replaced by the new man."[3] The apostle then grounds this reality of the new self and its new qualities in the sovereign election of God.

Chosen and Separate

The Apostle Paul addresses the Colossian church, "So, as those who have been chosen of God, holy and beloved" (3:12a). Paul uses the Greek word *eklektoi*, which is translated, "chosen," or, "chosen ones" to describe their status before God. This Greek word means, "Chosen as a recipient of special privilege, elect."[4] It is noteworthy that the apostle writes that the Colossians are "chosen of God," which conflicts with the corporate view of election that states only Christ is the chosen of God. The Colossians are "God's elect." Hendriksen translates this text as, "Put on, therefore, as God's elect, holy and beloved."[5] Greg Beale writes, "The phrase 'elect ones of God' is a subjunctive genitive meaning 'elected by God.'"[6] This is a demonstration of the personal nature of election by God. God chose them personally to be the recipients of the special privilege of being His people, and thereby to be holy and blameless.

As the elect of God, the Colossians are "to 'clothe themselves' with the lifestyle characteristics of the new creation in

---

[2] John MacArthur, *Colossians and Philemon*, MacNTC (Chicago: Moody Publishers, 1992), 148.

[3] MacArthur, *Colossians and Philemon*, MacNTC, 148-49.

[4] Mounce, *Analytical Lexicon to the Greek New Testament*, 172.

[5] William Hendriksen, *Colossians*, NTC (Grand Rapids: Baker Academic, 2007), 155.

[6] Greg Beale, *Colossians and Philemon*, BECNT (Grand Rapids: Baker Academic, 2019), 516.

Christist."[7] The apostle says of them that they are "holy and beloved" (v. 12). The first adjective to describe the Colossians is *hagioi* ("holy ones") from the Greek word *hagios*, which "fundamentally signifies 'separated,' and hence, in Scripture in its moral and spiritual significance, separated from sin and therefore consecrated to God, sacred."[8] MacArthur writes that believers are "holy" in that they are "set apart" or "separate." He adds, "God chose believers out of the mainstream of mankind and drew them to himself. When believers fail to act differently from the world, they violate the very purpose of their calling."[9] Hendriksen states that election affects the whole of the Christian life and is not simply an abstract idea. He states, "Although it belongs to the God's decree from eternity, it becomes a dynamic force in the hearts and lives of God's children. It produces fruits."[10]

The second adjective the apostle uses to describe the Colossians is *ēgapēmenoi* ("beloved"). Murray Harris writes, "God is the implied agent," thus, the meaning implied by this word is "loved by God," "his beloved," or "those on whom God set his love."[11] The meaning of this word also demonstrates the individual nature of salvation, namely, that God chose to set his love on individuals that he has elected and separated. This does not deny that God's love is granted to believers because of them being in Christ. As Beale states, "They are 'beloved' because of their identification with Christ, who is God's 'beloved Son.'"[12] God certainly loves all who are in Christ because of the work Christ accomplished on their behalf, and it is equally true that all who are in Christ are personally chosen to be in him by the Father. God did not set His love on them because he foresaw them believing in Christ, and thereby doing so because they loved him. That is a

---

[7] Beale, *Colossians and Philemon*, BECNT, 515.

[8] Vines, *Vines Complete Expository Dictionary*, 1825.

[9] Vines, *Vines Complete Expository Dictionary*, 154.

[10] Hendriksen, *Colossians*, NTC, 155.

[11] Murray Harris, *Colossians and Philemon*, EGGNT (Nashville: Baker Academic, 2010), 215.

[12] Beale, *Colossians and Philemon*, BECNT, 516.

conditional love, and it is only a response to them loving Christ first. The Scripture teaches quite the opposite: "We love, because he first loved us" (1 John 4:19). The qualities that Paul commands of the Colossians, who are chosen, holy, and beloved, are qualities that we find in God himself toward His elect.

The apostle lists five qualities that the believers are to "put on" as those whom are God's chosen: "heart of compassion, kindness, humility, gentleness, and patience." R. C. Lucas writes, "All of the five terms that describe the new man's conduct are used in other passages to designate acts of God or of Christ."[13] All five of these terms overlap and bring out similar meanings. The apostle first speaks of "a heart of compassion" or "bowels of compassion." This Greek word is from the root *oiktirmos*, which means, "compassion, kindness, in relieving sorrow and want."[14] The apostle uses the root word *oiktirmos* to describe the Lord in 2 Corinthians 1:3: "Blessed be the God and Father of our Lord Jesus Christ, the Father of *mercies* and God of all comfort" (emphasis added). David Garland says of Paul's use of this phrase that he "implies that mercies and comfort are brought to realization through Christ."[15] He adds, "The God to whom Paul offers up praise is not known only through theological theorems and creeds but through his direct action of comforting and showing mercy."[16] God's compassion is understood clearly through Christ's work on behalf of sinners. The Apostle Paul writes, "For while we were still helpless, at the right time, Christ died for the ungodly" (Rom 5:6). Williams Hendriksen states that we were powerless, helpless; meaning, totally unable to rescue ourselves from the effects of the Fall. Christ, however, being motivated out of sovereign love, died for us.[17] The Lord is the compassionate One who blots out our transgressions (Ps 51:1). It is the kindness

---

[13] R. C. Lucas, *The Message of Colossians and Philemon*, BST (Downers Grove: InterVarsity Press, 1980), 150.

[14] Mounce, *Analytical Lexicon to the Greek New Testament*, 336.

[15] David Garland, *2 Corinthians*, NAC (Grand Rapids: Zondervan, 1998), 59.

[16] Garland, *2 Corinthians*, NAC, 59.

[17] William Hendriksen, *Romans*, NTC (Grand Rapids: Baker Academic, 2007), 172.

of the Lord that leads us to repentance (Rom 2:4). He is long-suffering and patient (2 Pet 3:9), and he is gentle and lowly (Matt 11:29). When the Lord's goodness passed by Moses in Exodus 34:6, he proclaimed, "The Lord, the Lord God, compassionate and gracious, slow to anger, and abounding in lovingkindness and truth." The Lord Jesus proclaimed in Matthew 11:28–30, "Come to Me, all who are weary and heavy-laden, and I will give you rest. Take My yoke upon you and learn from Me, for I am gentle and humble in heart, and you will find rest for your souls. For My yoke is easy and My burden is light." In these two Scriptures alone contain all the characteristics that the apostle commands believers to put into practice—characteristics that are grounded in God's gracious nature toward His people.

Grounded in God's Character

The basis of all the qualities spoken of by Paul in Colossians 3:12–14 is the Lord himself and His gift of salvation to sinners. Hendriksen states, "Paul here links his admonitions to Christ's person and work. The qualities which, according to Paul's teaching here, mark the new man are also ascribed to Christ."[18] Paul speaks of putting on love, which is the perfect bond of unity (3:14). It was out of love that the Lord chose His elect before the foundation of the world. The Apostle Paul says in Ephesians 1:4b–5, "In love he predestined us to adoption as sons through Jesus Christ to himself according to the kind intention of His will." MacArthur writes, "That believers are beloved of God means they are objects of His special love. Election is not a cold, fatalistic

---

[18] Hendriksen, *Colossians*, NTC, 158. He writes, "This would seem to be the proper place to point out that Paul here links his admonitions to Christ's person and work, as has been indicated also in connection with Col 1:28. These qualities which, according to Paul's teaching here, mark the new man are also ascribed to Christ. For his 'heart of compassion' and his kindness, Matt 9:36; 14:14; 15:32; 20:34. His lowliness and meekness are exemplified in Matt 11:29; 21:5; John 13:1–15; Phil 2:8; his longsuffering and endurance or forbearance, in Matt 17:17; John 14:9; 1 Peter 2:23; and his forgiving spirit, in Matt 9:2; Luke 7:47; 23:34."

doctrine. On the contrary, it is based in God's incomprehensible love for His elect."[19] Believers are beloved of God for no other reason than God chose to bestow His love according to the kind intention of His will (Eph 1:5). He had compassion on us while we were yet sinners in rebellion against him (Rom 5:8); he calls us to himself out of a pure act of grace, and is patient toward us as we strive to walk accordingly and often fail. The qualities that the apostle commands the Colossians to practice have their reference point in the Lord, and as members of the family of God—holy and beloved—we are to "be imitators of God as beloved children" (Eph 5:1). The biblical doctrine of election magnifies the gracious qualities of God toward sinful rebels whom he has granted mercy.

What is the Difference?

How does the above view affect one's sanctification any more than a Arminian Christian's view? The qualities of "a heart of compassion, kindness, humility, gentleness, and patience" are greatly magnified even further in God through His gracious, unconditional election of sinners. For example, if one believes that God chose His elect based on what he foresaw or what he knew beforehand, then salvation would be granted based on a condition accomplished by the sinner. This implies that unless the sinner had met God's condition, then God would not have been gracious to save him. This is identifiable with the often-stated phrase, "God helps those who help themselves." If God only shows kindness, mercy, and grace to those who meet conditions, then on what basis would the child of God be any different toward others?

It is when we view salvation rightly, that God's compassion, kindness, gentleness, and patience are truly seen in light of God's unconditional election of those who hated him and rebelled against him. God would be perfectly just in condemning all, but God decided to show mercy. He did not show mercy on those who

---

[19] MacArthur, *Colossians and Philemon*, MacNTC, 154.

were kind toward him, but to sinful children of wrath: "But God, being rich in mercy, because of His great love with which he loved us, even when we were dead in our transgressions, made us alive together with Christ (by grace you have been saved)" (Eph 2:4). When Christians view God's unconditional election of sinners, then they have a solid foundation to be truly and unconditionally compassionate and kind toward all.

Questions for Reflection

1. Do you understand that God not only chose Christ Jesus, but has also chosen you?
2. Do you agree that the purpose of your calling by God is to be altogether separate from the world?
3. Do you see these qualities as those which God has shown towards you first?
4. Do you agree with the statement: "Election is not a cold, fatalistic doctrine." Why or why not?
5. How has your growth in Christ been affected by your knowledge of God's gracious character?

Chapter Eleven
Foundation for Obedience

"The assurance of election is a significant means whereby sanctification is promoted. . . . This is the daily experience of the godly. The more they are assured of the love of God towards them, the more they are stirred up to love God in return."[1]

The doctrine of election is our foundation for obedience unto the Lord. The gracious election of God granted to sinners should stir their affections to obey Christ, or said another way, to "walk in a manner worthy of the calling with which you have been called" (Eph 4:1). The Apostle Peter establishes this truth in 1 Peter 1:1–2 when he writes to the recipients of his epistle, "To those who reside as aliens . . . who are chosen according to the foreknowledge of God the Father, by the sanctifying work of the Spirit, to obey Jesus Christ and be sprinkled with His blood." Those in Christ are no longer their own but chosen by the Father, sanctified by the Spirit, and won through the victorious work of Jesus. The obedience of God's people is grounded in their election by the Father, sanctification by the Spirit, and redemption by Christ Jesus. They have been purchased not "with perishable things like silver or gold . . . but with precious blood, as of a lamb unblemished and spotless, the blood of Christ" (1 Pet 1:18–19). This truth is also taught by the Apostle Paul: "Or do you not know that your body is a temple of the Holy Spirit who is in you, whom you have from God, and that you are not your own? For you have been bought with a price; therefore glorify God in your body" (1 Cor 6:19–20). Obedience is grounded in God's electing sinners to receive the gift of redemption wrought by the Lord Jesus.

---

[1] á Brakel, *Christian's Reasonable Service*, 250.

The reality of God's election and redemption as the basis for the obedience of God's people is not only a New Testament idea. The Old Covenant also teaches this same truth. The Lord says to the people of Israel, "The Lord your God has chosen you to be a people for His own possession out of all the peoples who are on the face of the earth" (Deut 7:6). It is important to note that God chose them to be His people and redeemed them as a result. R. C. Sproul states the following:

> God certainly cares about our following His commandments. Yet there is more to the story that we dare not forget. God gave laws such as the Ten Commandments in the context of the covenant. First, God was gracious. He redeemed His people out of slavery in Egypt and entered into a loving, filial relationship with Israel. Only after that grace-based relationship was established did God begin to define the specific laws that are pleasing to him.[2]

When we read the Ten Commandments in Exodus 20:1-17, for example, we see that these are not simply commands by God to obey, but are commands to obey as the result of God's gracious act of redemption. Chapter 20 of the book of Exodus begins, "Then God spoke all these words, saying, 'I am the Lord your God, who brought you out of the land of Egypt, out of the house of slavery'" (20:1-2). This is repeated in Deuteronomy 5:6, and the Lord also says in Leviticus 25:55, "For the sons of Israel are My servants; they are My servants whom I brought out from the land of Egypt. I am the Lord your God." About this cause-and-effect relationship, John Calvin states,

> In these words, then, God seeks to procure reverence to himself, before he prescribes the rule of a holy and righteous life. Moreover, he not merely declares himself to be Jehovah, the only God to whom men are bound by the right of creation, who has given them their existence, and who preserves their

---

[2] R. C. Sproul, *How Can I Develop a Christian Conscience* (Orlando, FL: Reformation Trust, 2013), 37.

life, nay, who is himself the life of all; but he adds, that he is the peculiar God of the Israelites; for it was expedient, not only that the people should be alarmed by the majesty of God, but also that they should be gently attracted, so that the law might be more precious than gold and silver, and at the same time "sweeter than honey," (Psalms 119:72) for it would not be enough for men to be compelled by servile fear to bear its yoke, unless they were also attracted by its sweetness, and willingly endured it. He afterwards recounts that special blessing, wherewith he had honored the people, and by which he had testified that they were not elected by him in vain; for their redemption was the sure pledge of their adoption. But, in order to bind them the better to himself, he reminds them also of their former condition; for Egypt was like a house of bondage, from whence the Israelites were delivered. Wherefore, they were no more their own masters, since God had purchased them unto himself.[3]

The basis of God's commands to Israel was His gracious act of choosing them to be His people and redeeming them from slavery in Egypt, and this is the same teaching the Apostle Peter puts forth in 1 Peter 1:1–2.

Chosen according to the Foreknowledge of God the Father

The doctrine of election manifests the gracious nature of God in the salvation of sinners and is motivation for godly living. David Walls and Max Anders write, "In themselves, believers are just ordinary people, but the gracious choice of God makes us what we are—the ones whom God favors and loves."[4] The expla-

---

[3] John Calvin, *Harmony of Exodus, Leviticus, Numbers, Deuteronomy*, CC (Grand Rapids: Baker Books, 2009), 339.

[4] David Walls and Max Anders, *I Peter*, HNTC (Nashville: Holman Reference, 1999), 6.

nation brings out the initial nuance of Peter, namely, that believers are chosen and are loved, for the apostle states that the recipients are "chosen of God according to the foreknowledge of God the Father" (v. 1). The word "chosen" (*eklektois*) in this text is the same word, though a different form, from *eklektoi* in Colossians 3:12, which means, "chosen as a recipient of special privilege, elect."[5] The Scripture, again, teaches the personal election of God's people. The Father chose Peter's audience for a special privilege, namely, salvation through Christ. This is also what we learned from the Apostle Paul in Ephesians 1:3–6: "He [the Father] chose us in him [Christ]" (Eph 1:4).

God's love for those he chose in Christ is also implied by Peter's use of the word "foreknowledge." "Foreknowledge" (*prognōsin*), from *prognosis*, means, "previous determination, purpose."[6] Karen Jobes writes, "Peter reminds his readers that the God who took the initiative in their lives has drawn them into an intimate, loving, and redemptive relationship with him, but also one in which God claims supreme authority over their lives."[7] In other words, the foreknowledge of God that is spoken of in this text is neither a general knowledge that God has of every human being, nor a simple foresight of those who would believe. Rather, it is an intimate love that God has toward His own. Michael Reeves writes that the love that God the Father has for God the Son is the same love that the Father has for all who are in the Son.[8] The subject of God's foreknowledge will be discussed further in the section on Romans 8:28–30.

---

[5] Mounce, *Analytical Lexicon to the Greek New Testament*, 172.

[6] Mounce, *Analytical Lexicon to the Greek New Testament*, 390.

[7] Karen Jobes, *1 Peter*, BECNT (Grand Rapids: Baker Academic, 2005), 69.

[8] Michael Reeves, *Delighting in the Trinity* (Downers Grove: IVP Academic, 2012), 75. He writes, "When the Spirit rested upon the Son at His baptism, Jesus heard the Father declare from heaven: 'You are my Son, whom I love; with you I am well pleased.' But now that the same Spirit of sonship rests on me, the same words apply to me: in Christ my high priest I am an adopted, beloved, Spirit-anointed son. As Jesus says to the Father in John 17:23, you 'have loved them even as you have loved me.' And so, as the Son brings me before His Father, with their Spirit in me I can boldly cry, 'Abba,' for their fellowship I now freely

Obedience Grounded in Election

The Apostle Peter recounts to his audience who are enduring fiery trials of their election from the Lord, and the result of that election which is obedience. Matthew Henry writes, "All that are chosen to eternal life as the end are chosen to obedience as the way. Unless a person be sanctified by the Spirit, and sprinkled with the blood of Jesus, there will be no true obedience in the life."[9] Again, the command to obey is not simply a cold command by a despot, but a command by a loving God who rescued His elect from His necessary wrath over their sin. Charles Hodge writes, "We were justly held in bondage. We were under the penalty of the law, and until that law was satisfied, we could not be delivered."[10] He adds that since redemption has come through such a high price as the blood of Christ, we are to honor him and "so act as to cause him to be honored by others."[11] Peter alludes to the work of redemption when he writes, "and be sprinkled with His blood" (v. 2). The Greek word *rhantismon* (sprinkled) means, "A cleansing, a purification."[12] Vines states that this word is "an allusion to the use of the blood sacrifices, appointed for Israel, typical of the sacrifice of Christ."[13] The God who delivered us from the bondage sin and has granted to us eternal life, now commands believers to "walk in a manner worthy of the calling with which you have been called" (Eph 4:1).

---

share: the Most High my Father, the Son my great brother, the Spirit no longer Jesus's Comforter alone, but mine."

[9] Matthew Henry, *Matthew Henry's Commentary on the Whole Bible* (Peabody, MA: Hendrickson Publishers, 1991), 2422.

[10] Hodge, *I & II Corinthians*, 106.

[11] Hodge, *I & II Corinthians*, 106.

[12] Mounce, *Analytical Lexicon to the Greek New Testament*, 406.

[13] Vines, *Complete Expository Dictionary*, 2751

The Sanctifying Spirit

Peter goes on to state that not only are believers chosen according to God's choice to elect those upon whom he desires to bestow His divine love, but he does so by the sanctifying work of the Holy Spirit (*en hagiasmō pneumatos*, v. 2). This sanctifying work of the Spirit of God produces the effect of obedience to Christ. Jobes writes, "When the purpose of the work of the Spirit—given in the third prepositional phrase—is considered, the sanctification in view here is first the consecration of these people that occurred when they heard and responded to the word of God effectively preached in the power of the Spirit, which brought forth their new birth."[14] Jobes goes on to state,

> This consecrating work of the Spirit has a specific purpose. He does not bring a person to some generic spirituality, such as is currently popular in much of Western culture, but more specifically into the new covenant founded on the blood of Christ Jesus. The Christians to whom Peter writes were chosen in God's foreknowledge by the work of the Spirit for a purpose. In our spiritually pluralistic society, many today believe in a supreme God and speak of his Spirit working in the lives of his people. But Peter drives home the point that the people to whom he writes were chosen for the distinct purpose of "obedience and sprinkling of the blood of Jesus Christ," not simply for some generic form of spirituality.[15]

The reality of a Christian's obedience is intimately connected in the redemptive work of Christ, and flows from the election of the Father through the sanctification of the Holy Spirit. Matthew Henry writes, "God's decree for man's salvation always operates through sanctification of the Spirit and sprinkling of the blood of Jesus."[16] The sprinkling of the blood of Christ reflects back to the

---

[14] Jobes, *1 Peter*, BECNT, 70.

[15] Jobes, *1 Peter*, BECNT, 70.

[16] Henry, *Matthew Henry's Commentary*, 2421.

purification rites of Israel in Numbers 19. The idea being conveyed is the cleansing that is received through Christ that brings about one's justification. John Calvin states, "There is then to be understood here a contrast, that, as formerly under the law the sprinkling of blood was made by the hand of the priest; so now the Holy Spirit sprinkles our souls with the blood of Christ for the expiation of our sins."[17] The sanctifying work of the Spirit of God is summed up by Calvin in the following words:

> Our salvation flows from the gratuitous election of God; but that it is to be ascertained by the experience of faith, because he sanctifies us by his Spirit; and then that there are two effects or ends of our calling, even renewal into obedience and ablution by the blood of Christ; further, that both are the work of the Holy Spirit. We hence conclude, that election is not to be separated from calling, nor the gratuitous righteousness of faith from newness of life.[18]

The Holy Spirit applies all the benefits of the work of Christ to the believer. Steve Lawson writes with reference to 1 Peter 1:2, "In the original language, the word translated as 'sanctification' means 'to separate' or 'to consecrate.' It refers here to all the Spirit does in the salvation of the elect. This saving ministry includes the Spirit's work of convicting of sin, drawing to Christ, producing regeneration, granting repentance, and bestowing saving faith."[19]

The election of God that is brought about by the Spirit of God results in the outward manifestation of faith, which is obedience to Christ. What is it that Peter refers to here? The apostle explains further: "As obedient children, do not be conformed to the former lusts which were yours in your ignorance, but like the Holy One who called you, be holy yourselves also in all your behavior; because it is written, 'You shall be holy, for I am holy'" (1:14–16). Walls and Anders write that "obedience" is the idea of

---

[17] John Calvin, *1 Peter*, CC (Grand Rapids: Baker Books, 2009), 26.

[18] Calvin, *1 Peter*, CC, 26–27.

[19] Lawson, *Foundations of Grace*, 323.

listening and submitting to the Word of God, and involves a change of attitude in the believer from his former thoughts and attitude.[20]

They go on to state, "We obey the call of Jesus to salvation, the word of Jesus in the Bible, and the encouragement of Jesus found in personal relationship with him each day."[21] Our Lord Jesus himself stated in John 14:15, "If you love Me, you will keep My commandments," and, "My Father is glorified by this, that you bear much fruit, and so prove to be My disciples" (15:8). The Scriptures continually emphasize that true believers will bear fruit or walk worthy of Christ. God's election in Christ leads toward good works, for this is what the apostle states: "According to the foreknowledge of God the Father, by the sanctifying work of the Spirit, to obey Jesus Christ" (1 Pet 1:2). Grudem states, "For obedience to Jesus Christ indicates God's purpose in the readers' present existence as 'chosen sojourners' in their native lands: their lives ought to be leading 'toward' (*eis*) increasing obedience to Christ. What the Father plans, the Spirit empowers, and Christ is thus received as the exalted Savior and ruling Lord."[22]

Be Holy for I Am Holy

Our obedience to the Lord Jesus is grounded in the Father's election of Christ's bride. Just as the election of God's people in the Old Testament that resulted in redemption was the basis for their obedience, so too, the same is true for all believers since the coming of Christ. God has saved us, called us, and has ordained us to walk in the newness of life. It is important to note that Peter speaks in the same manner of New Testament believers as the Old Testament Scriptures spoke of Israel. God chose to set His love on Israel and redeem them (Deut 7:6–7), and this is the reality under the New Covenant. As expounded in the previous sections, election is personal and unconditional, and this grace of

---

[20] Walls and Anders, *I Peter*, HNTC, 7.

[21] Walls and Anders, *I Peter*, HNTC, 7.

[22] Wayne Grudem, *1 Peter*, TNTC (Downers Grove: IVP Academic), 56.

God results in the redemption of all the Father chose before the foundation of the world (Eph 1:4, 7). The people of God under the New Covenant no more chose God to be their God than the people under the Old Covenant, though there are differences to be sure of physical (redemption from Egypt) vs. spiritual redemption (redemption from sin). The same result occurs in both: obedience unto the Lord. The Apostle Paul states in Ephesians 2:10, "For we are His workmanship, created in Christ Jesus for good works, which God prepared beforehand so that we would walk in them." The Apostle Peter emphasizes the same with his reference to God's command to "be holy as he is holy." As Grudem states,

> As he who called you is holy means according to the way or manner in which God is holy, you yourselves are to be holy, patterning your holiness after his. Peter reminds his readers that it was God who initiated their salvation when the gospel came to them in power, summoning them out of darkness into fellowship with himself. It was a powerful, effectual calling into the Christian life and all it involves—a calling to live with God and to be like him.[23]

MacArthur would write that the doctrine of election is a powerful incentive to holy living. He says, "Knowing God has set them apart because of His own special love for them is a most effective motivation for believers to love to the glory of God. Their gratitude to God for His election of them should compel believers to a life of obedience and holiness."[24]

The reality of Peter's words results in a greater degree of affection resulting in obedience. The affection for God deepens when it is understood more clearly that God's predetermined love upon believers, brought to them by the Spirit of God, and secured by the work of Christ, was not the result of any foresight

---

[23] Grudem, *1 Peter*, TNTC, 85.

[24] John MacArthur, *1 Peter*, MacNTC (Chicago: Moody Publishers, 2004), 27.

of potential atonement, but by a pure act of grace. This truth produces a greater degree of love for God than that of simply believing that God made a way to Christ but secured no true redemption for them unless they choose God. The previous sections have attempted to demonstrate that mankind apart from God's regenerating work will never come to him (John 6:44, 65), and therefore, simply making a way to Christ results in no actual effect. However, as 1 Peter 1:1–2 teaches, knowing that God loved beforehand a particular people he chose to save, sent Christ to redeem them, and sent the Holy Spirit to sanctify them, moves the affections of God's people even more to live a life that pleases our gracious God and Savior. Our election in Christ is the foundation for greater, more genuine, and heartfelt obedience to the Lord.

Questions for Reflection

1. Does the knowledge of God's gracious election of you stir you to obey him?
2. Do you agree that obedience to God is grounded in His sovereign election of you? Why or why not?
3. Do you agree that election is a motivation for heartfelt, godly living?
4. Do you see God's foreknowledge, not simply as foresight, but as an intimate love God has for His own?
5. Do you see God as a loving Rescuer of your soul or as a cold despot demanding obedience?

Chapter Twelve
Emboldened for Evangelism

"The cause of any person believing is the will of God; and the outward sound of the Gospel strikes the ear but in vain until God is pleased to touch the heart within."[1]

In His Great Commission, our Lord Jesus commanded His disciples to go into all the world and preach the gospel. This mandate to the apostles has been understood to be a command to all believers in every age. William Hendriksen writes that when the Lord commands them to "go," "it implies that the disciples—and this holds for God's children in general—must not concentrate all their thought on 'coming' to church. They must also 'go' to bring the precious tidings to others."[2] This command of the Lord has been met with various degrees of opposition and persecution. The Apostle Paul himself suffered greatly for the sake of the gospel. As he states in 2 Corinthians 11:24–27, he received lashes on five different occasions, shipwrecked three times, stoned once, three times beaten with rods, and in constant danger from his own countrymen and from the Gentiles. His imprisonment was also for the sake of the gospel (Phil 1:13).

In spite of all these hardships, the Apostle Paul continued to declare the gospel of Christ for the sake of the elect of God. He states in Titus 1:1, "Paul, a bondservant of God and an apostle of Jesus Christ, for the faith of those chosen of God and the knowledge of the truth which is according to godliness." In other words, part of Paul's mission was the evangelization of the elect of God. MacArthur writes of Paul's words in Titus 1:1, "Paul first

---

[1] Boettner, *Reformed Doctrine of Predestination*, 359.

[2] William Hendriksen, *Matthew*, NTC (Grand Rapids: Baker Academic, 2007), 999.

recognized his responsibility to help bring God's elect, those who are chosen of God, to saving faith in Jesus Christ."[3] Paul writes to Timothy to fulfill the same mission that was given to him, and to all of the people of God, and the grounds of Paul's encouragement to Timothy is the sovereign, unconditional election of God.

The Setting of 2 Timothy

In his second letter to Timothy, written about AD 66, the Apostle Paul writes again to his child in the faith to give him encouragement during the period of persecution under Emperor Nero as he pastored the church at Ephesus. Hendriksen writes that comfort was certainly needed during that period of raging persecution, that Timothy would not lose heart or fear death, but that his confidence would be in the One who conquered the enemy.[4] MacArthur adds, "The church at Ephesus had fallen still further into corrupt theology and ungodly behavior. Church leaders, including Timothy to some extent, were even weaker and less effective than when 1 Timothy was written. Heresy, apostasy, and even persecution had become more destructive."[5] MacArthur further states, "Paul wanted Timothy to fully understand that he, like the apostle himself, was under divine compulsion as a minister of Jesus Christ. . . . Paul wanted Timothy to understand that these were not merely suggestions from a loving friend and adviser but were divinely inspired commands from an apostle of the Lord Jesus Christ."[6]

---

[3] John MacArthur, *Titus*, MacNTC (Chicago: Moody Publishers, 1996), 4.

[4] William Hendriksen, *2 Timothy*, NTC (Grand Rapids: Baker Academic, 2007), 250.

[5] John MacArthur, *2 Timothy*, MacNTC (Chicago: Moody Publishers, 1995), x.

[6] MacArthur, *2 Timothy*, MacNTC, xi.

Called Us with a Holy Calling

The Apostle Paul gives Timothy numerous imperatives throughout the epistle. However, in chapter 2, the apostle addresses Timothy regarding his need to suffer hardship as a good soldier of Christ (2:3). In suffering for Christ, Timothy must focus on the preeminence of Jesus and the purpose for which he suffers. Paul commands Timothy to "remember Jesus Christ, risen from the dead, descendent of David, according to my gospel, for which I suffer hardship even to imprisonment as a criminal" (2:8-9a). It is in the verses of 2:8-13 where the apostle expounds to Timothy the purpose of his hardship, and the encouragement to continue to declare the gospel of Christ in order that the chosen of God may obtain the salvation that is in Christ Jesus. The foundation of this command is given in Pauls' words earlier in his second epistle to Timothy.

Paul opened his epistle with a reminder to Timothy of God's sovereign grace that was granted to him. He states, "Therefore, do not be ashamed of the testimony of our Lord or of me His prisoner, but join with me in suffering for the gospel according to the power of God, who has saved us and called us with a holy calling, not according to our works, but according to His own purpose and grace which was granted us in Christ Jesus from all eternity" (1:8-9). Paul's encouragement to Timothy is, "Do not be ashamed of the testimony of our Lord" (v. 8). The word "ashamed" (*epaischunthēs*) carries the meaning, as Köstenberger and Thomas point out, that Timothy "must not avoid the shame of being identified with a crucified criminal (Jesus), he must not shrink back from the social stigma attached to being associated with the imprisoned Paul."[7] In other words, regardless of what persecution may await Timothy for his commitment to Christ or his solidarity with Paul, Timothy must not give in to fear and be silent to avoid such trying times. He is to be bold in the Lord, "For God has not given us a spirit of timidity, but of power and love and discipline" (v. 7). He is to suffer for the gospel as Paul himself

---

[7] Robert L. Thomas and Andreas Köstenberger, *2 Timothy*, EBC (Grand Rapids: Zondervan, 2006), 368.

was doing. Robert Gundry states, "Association with a crucified Christ and with Paul, imprisoned for preaching that such a Christ is Lord, might well make Timothy ashamed to carry forward Paul's extension of the Lord's testimony. But because God has given Christians, such as Paul and Timothy, the Spirit of power, love, and sensibility, Timothy shouldn't be ashamed to carry it forward."[8]

Paul reminds Timothy of the sovereign call of God that was determined in eternity past. Paul states, "[God] has saved us and called us with a holy calling, not according to our works, but according to His own purpose and grace which was granted us in Christ Jesus from all eternity" (v. 9). Hendriksen writes, "Salvation is not based on our accomplishments but on God's sovereign purpose, his wise, fixed, and definite plan; and therefore on his grace or sovereign favor."[9] Hendriksen further writes that this grace precedes our works as a result of the elect being its object before time began.[10] It is here that the Apostle Paul sets the foundation of the epistle with the reality of the doctrine of election. As Hendriksen points out, "Time, like an ever-rolling stream, flows on and on and on. But before it even began we were already included in the gracious purpose of God."[11] Gundry adds the following:

> "Not in accordance with our works" means that no good deeds which we might have done, or which God foresaw we would do, had anything to do with God's calling us with a holy calling. The calling had to do solely with God's "purpose and grace," the independence of which purpose and grace from "our works" is accented by "his own." "Which was given to us in Christ Jesus" describes God's grace as a gift encapsulated in the person and work of Christ Jesus. But God gave us his grace in the past eternity [*pro chronon aiōniōn*] ("before

[8] Robert H. Gundry, *Commentary on First and Second Timothy, Titus* (Grand Rapids: Baker Academic, 2010), 51.

[9] Hendriksen, *2 Timothy*, NTC, 232.

[10] Hendriksen, *2 Timothy*, NTC, 232.

[11] Hendriksen, *2 Timothy*, NTC, 232–33.

times eternal"), because that's when he purposed to call us with a holy calling.[12]

Paul reminds Timothy of God's electing purposes and the grace shown to sinners through this act of God. It was a reminder, but even more so, Paul wrote of it as an encouragement to a possibly intimidated Timothy.

Motives for Ministry

In light of the difficult circumstances that Timothy was enduring, the Apostle Paul encourages Timothy to "remember Jesus Christ, risen from the dead, descendant of David, according to my gospel" (2:8). Paul commands Timothy to "remember." This Greek word *mnēmoneue* means, "recollect, call to mind; to be mindful of, to fix thoughts upon."[13] The apostle is saying, "Timothy, fix your thoughts upon Christ, His victorious resurrection that is central to the faith which secured your salvation, who is the fulfillment of all prophecy, according to the truths of God's good news declared to you." Donald Guthrie explains it as follows:

> The words *Remember Jesus Christ, raised from the dead*, draw attention to the present experience of the risen Lord, which would be particularly underlined by Paul's own conversion. It is not so much the resurrection as a fact of history, important as that is, but the risen Christ as the central factor of the Christian's ongoing experience. For Paul the resurrection is the most prominent Christian truth, containing as it does the guarantee of all other aspects of the work of Christ.[14]

The great encouragement to Timothy is to remember the risen Lord, because as he lives and was resurrected, so too, all in

[12] Gundry, *2 Timothy*, 52.

[13] Mounce, *Analytical Lexicon to the Greek New Testament*, 322.

[14] Donald Guthrie, *The Pastoral Epistles*, TNTC, vol. 14 (Downers Grove: IVP Academic, 2015), 136.

Christ will be raised from the dead. The implication is that Christ having been raised from the dead is alive, and that "we do not serve a past event or a merely historical person . . . we worship and serve him because he is no longer dead but alive."[15] This Christ Jesus, who is truly God and truly man, who was raised from the dead, is whom Timothy must focus upon during his hardships. MacArthur states, "As our sovereign Lord, Jesus Christ controls everything that we are and everything that happens to us. We must resist temptation, but we need not fear it."[16] The Apostle Paul himself at this time was enduring hardship "even to imprisonment as a criminal" (v. 9). Gundry writes, "The 'hard-' in 'hardship' connotes harm, injury. Accenting this connotation is a wordplay, *kakopathō . . . hōs kakourgos*, which when translated literally comes out as 'suffering bad . . . as a doer of bad.'"[17] However, he looks to the great comfort that "his imprisonment did not hinder the gospel from having free course; and not only so, but that what he suffers is advantageous to the elect, because it tends to confirm them."[18] His main focus was upon Christ and edifying the body of Christ.

As Paul encourages Timothy, he writes these words: "For this reason I endure all things for the sake of those who are chosen, so that they also may obtain the salvation which is in Christ Jesus and with it eternal glory" (v. 10). The word "chosen" (*eklektous*) is from the same root word *eklektos* used in Colossians 3:12 and 1 Peter 1:1, meaning, "chosen as a recipient of special privilege, elect."[19] Lawson writes, "As Paul suffered his imprisonment in Rome, he remained confident that the sovereign purposes of God could never be impeded. This truth made him resolute in the ministry and triumphant in his outlook, even in the face of difficult circumstances. This was because the doctrine of sovereign election is a soul-anchoring, faith-building truth."[20] The doctrine

[15] MacArthur, *2 Timothy*, MacNTC, 56–57.

[16] MacArthur, *2 Timothy*, MacNTC, 57.

[17] Gundry, *Commentary on First and Second Timothy, Titus*, 57.

[18] John Calvin, *2 Timothy*, CC (Grand Rapids: Baker Books, 2009), 215.

[19] Mounce, *Analytical Lexicon to the Greek New Testament*, 172.

[20] Lawson, *Foundations of Grace*, 451.

of election emboldened the apostle to continue preaching the gospel and enduring all the hardships. Paul was willing "to bear up under or/and suffer patiently"[21] hardships for the elect (v. 10). The phrase, "for the sake of those who are chosen," according to Guthrie, "seems to mean those who are elect but do not yet believe. They have to be won and every ounce of effort must be put into this conflict."[22] It is also in this conflict or labor that Paul is encouraging Timothy to persevere. John Piper states, "Evangelism and missions are not imperiled by the biblical truth of election, but are empowered by it, and their triumph is secured by it."[23] Paul trusted in the sovereign election of God to bring His people to faith through the means of the gospel.

The Power of God unto Salvation

A very helpful example of this truth in practice is in Acts 18. Luke writes in Acts 18:5 that Paul in Corinth began devoting himself completely to the Word of God when Silas and Timothy came down from Macedonia. Paul was reasoning among the Jews every Sabbath, testifying that Jesus was the Christ. John Polhill writes that Paul was freed to minister more continually because of Silas and Timothy coming to Corinth. Polhill points out that the inevitable consequence of Paul's reasoning with the Jews was strong Jewish opposition.[24] Luke tells his readers that as a result of the Jews' strong opposition to the gospel, even to the extent that they blasphemed, "he [Paul] shook out his garments and said to them, 'Your blood be on your own heads! I am clean. From now on I will go to the Gentiles'" (Acts 18:6). The Lord appeared to Paul in a vision and said, "Do not be afraid any longer, but go on speaking and do not be silent; for I am with you, and no man will attack you in order to harm you, for I have many people in this

---

[21] Mounce, *Analytical Lexicon to the Greek New Testament*, 464.

[22] Guthrie, *The Pastoral Epistles*, TNTC, 137.

[23] John Piper, *The Pleasures of God* (Colorado Springs: Multnomah Books, 2012), 149.

[24] John Polhill, *Acts*, NAC (Nashville: B&H Publishing, 1992), 384.

city" (Acts 18:9–10). MacArthur states of this passage, "Here it is clear that some people belong to the Lord who are not yet saved, and they will not be saved without the preaching of the gospel. Paul defined his preaching as having the purpose of bringing the elect to faith."[25] Lawson writes that the elect Corinthians' salvation was so certain that God regarded them as His people before they were even saved, and adds, "This truth of divine election gave the apostle great courage to hold fast."[26]

Bold Proclamation

The experiences of the Apostle Paul prepared him not only to endure hardships himself, but also to encourage Timothy to do the same for the sake of the elect. Paul endured the Jewish opposition in Corinth for the elect's sake and stayed there another eighteen months preaching. His knowledge of God's sovereignty in the salvation of sinners emboldened him to keep preaching the gospel. Wayne Grudem writes of Paul's words in 2 Timothy 2:10: "He knows that God has chosen some people to be saved and he sees this as an encouragement to preach the gospel, even if it means enduring great suffering. Election is Paul's guarantee that there will be some success for his evangelism, for he knows that some of the people he speaks to will be the elect, and they will believe the gospel and be saved. It is as if someone invited us to come fishing and said, 'I guarantee that you will catch some fish—they are hungry and waiting.'"[27] The doctrine of election

---

[25] John MacArthur, *Acts*, MacNTC (Chicago: Moody Publishers, 1996), 151.

[26] Lawson, *Foundations of Grace*, 472. He writes, "Soon after Paul began ministering in Corinth, he became discouraged by the great opposition and many obstacles he faced. Filled with despair, the apostle was ready to move to another city that might be more receptive to the gospel. But God appeared to Paul in a vision and told him that He had many people in Corinth—a reference to His chosen ones, those who would believe once the truth was preached to them. This truth of divine election gave the apostle great courage to hold fast. The salvation of these chosen individuals was so certain, God regarded them as His people before they were even saved."

[27] Grudem, *Systematic Theology*, 674.

emboldened the Apostle Paul to keep evangelizing for the sake of the elect even in the face of persecution.

Paul's approach to evangelism was not one of relying on his own abilities to speak cleverly to convince a sinner (1 Cor 1:17). Paul relied on the gospel being "the power of God unto salvation for everyone who believes" (Rom 1:16). Evangelism for the apostle was not a matter of hoping that God was providing prevenient grace to bring a sinner to a neutral place to hear Paul's convincing presentation of the good news. As the Lord said to Paul in Acts 18:9–10, Paul was to keep preaching because the Lord's people, His elect, come to faith through the declaration of the gospel. As the apostle says in Romans 10:17, "So faith comes from hearing, and hearing by the word of Christ." Beeke writes, "Election compels evangelism, for all the elect must be saved by the Word brought to them."[28] Beeke goes on to state,

> We do not know how many people God has elected in our cities. We trust there are many. But many or few, they are the Lord's, and he has given us means to find them. So we must faithfully pray, speak, and visit people, always abounding in Christ's work and always ready to give a reason for the hope that is in us to anyone who asks (1 Pet 3:15).[29]

This truth of election is the foundation not only for Paul and Timothy, but for all believers to boldly carry out the Great Commission commanded by the Lord Jesus. Apart from this reality, the evangelist is left with his own devices and clever tactics to try on his own to bring others to Christ. For the evangelist, when the biblical doctrine of election is rejected, the responsibility of conversion is his, and the unbelieving person's rejection of Christ is his failure. Let us thank our Lord that this is not at all the truth we find in Scripture. It is God alone who saves by His mighty power and does so through the faithful proclamation of His gospel by His people.

---

[28] Beeke, *Living for God's Glory*, 70.

[29] Beeke, *Living for God's Glory*, 70.

Questions for Reflection

1. Do you recognize that the mandate of the Great Commission is for you also?
2. Do you avoid sharing the Gospel for fear of persecution?
3. Are your thoughts fixed upon Christ's power or your own abilities when sharing the Gospel?
4. Are you willing to experience hardship that others would come to know Christ?
5. Does the doctrine of election give you greater courage to declare the Gospel?

Chapter Thirteen
A Comfort in our Everyday Life

*"The basis upon which God elected . . . was not a faith foreseen . . .
because a choice founded upon the foresight of good works is just as truly
made on the ground of works as any choice can be, and in such a case, it
would not be of grace."*[1]

As taught throughout this chapter, the doctrine of election moves our hearts in genuine praise to God, crushes our pride, gives us a foundation of a Christ-like character, emboldens our evangelism, and gives us strength during our times of suffering. The biblical doctrine of election also provides us comfort throughout our everyday lives. Just as it provides strength during trials, so too, it provides comfort. Grudem writes, "The New Testament authors often present the doctrine of election as a comfort to believers."[2] This is seen in Paul's epistle to the Romans in chapter eight where the apostle writes,

> And we know that God causes all things to work together for good to those who love God, to those who are called according to His purpose. For those whom he foreknew, he also predestined to become conformed to the image of His Son, so that he would be the firstborn among many brethren; and these whom he predestined, he also called; and these whom he called, he also justified; and these whom he justified, he also glorified. (Rom 8:28–30)

These verses contain one of the most often quoted texts, which is verse 28, and it contains what is known as the golden chain of salvation, five particular blessings recorded in Romans 8:29–30.

---

[1] A.W. Pink, *The Sovereignty of God* (Carlisle: Banner of Truth, 2009) 44.

[2] Grudem, *Systematic Theology*, 673.

Sproul writes, "We notice a kind of order here that begins with God's foreknowledge and is carried through to the glorification of the believer."[3] The blessings of salvation not only include being predestined by God, but also being called, justified in the sight of God, and glorified. The apostle also emphasizes the sanctification of the believer in being conformed to the image of Christ which then culminates in glorification. This text once again connects the doctrine of election to the sanctification of the believer.

The Context of Romans 8

Throughout the epistle to the Romans Paul has labored in emphasizing several important truths such as justification by faith alone (3:2–5; 5:1), and he has pointed to the result of the believers' justification by faith (5:1–21; 6:17–18; 7:24–25). Here also, Paul emphasizes the result of justification by faith in chapter 8. Hendriksen writes, "The fact that justification is indeed at the center of Paul's thinking is clear from the opening words, 'There is now no condemnation,' for condemnation is the opposite of justification."[4] Throughout chapter 8 the apostle explains the effects of being justified. For example, those who have been justified walk "according to the Spirit" (v. 5), have put "to death the deeds of the body" (v. 13), "are being led by the Spirit of God" (v. 14), and "have not received a spirit of slavery leading to fear again, but . . . have received a spirit of adoption as sons" (v. 15). The apostle encourages his readers during their time of suffering saying, "For I consider that the sufferings of this present time are not worthy to be compared with the glory that is to be revealed to us" (v.18).

MacArthur writes, "Paul does not merely suggest, but strongly affirms, that any suffering for Christ's sake is a small price to pay for the gracious benefits received because of that

---

[3] Sproul, *Chosen by God,* 104.
[4] Hendriksen, *Romans,* NTC,

suffering."[5] As the apostle continues in chapter 8 of Romans, he then speaks of the Holy Spirit interceding for us when we do not know how to pray as we should. Paul writes,

> In the same way the Spirit also helps our weakness; for we do not know how to pray as we should, but the Spirit himself intercedes for us with groanings too deep for words; and he who searches the hearts knows what the mind of the Spirit is, because he intercedes for the saints according to the will of God. (Rom 8:26–27)

It is from this flow of thought where the apostle encourages believers of their hope in Christ as they endure their sufferings and struggles that he then says, "And we know that God causes all things to work together for good to those who love God, to those who are called according to His purpose" (Rom 8:28).

The Called of God: Romans 8:28

Romans 8:28 is a comforting passage that cannot be fully understood except in light of verses 1–27. As the apostle concludes his thoughts, he speaks this comforting truth of God's providence in the life of a believer. MacArthur writes, "For Christians, this verse contains perhaps the most glorious promise in Scripture. It is breathtaking in its magnitude, encompassing absolutely everything that pertains to a believer's life."[6] Thielman writes, "God orders the circumstances in which his people live so that these circumstances cooperate in bringing about his good purpose of delivering his people and creation from the effects of sin."[7] Hendriksen echoes this and adds that "evil designs are by

---

[5] John MacArthur, *Romans 1-8*, MacNTC (Chicago: Moody Publishers, 1991), 449.

[6] MacArthur, *Romans 1-8*, MacNTC, 471.

[7] Thielman, *Romans*, ECNT, 584.

God overruled for good."[8] The word *agathov*, from *agathos*, means, "good, profitable, generous, upright, virtuous."[9] Vines writes that "*agathos* describes that which, being 'good' in its character of constitution, is beneficial in its effect."[10] This would include the trials that the apostle had just expounded. God works or brings out good in trials. Thielman states, "There is no doubt that Paul understood God's 'purpose,' and therefore his will and power, to be the force that causes everything to work for good."[11]

The apostle writes, "All things work together for good to those who love God, to those who are called according to His purpose" (8:28). Schreiner provides the following commentary:

> To say that God works in everything for good "for those who love God (tois agapōsiv ton theon) should not be understood as a condition here, for even though the promise applies only to those who love God, the intention in using this phrase is not to distinguish true from false believers. Paul doesn't speak often of believers loving God, and here the phrase is another way of denoting those who are believers. . . . Thus Paul adds the phrase *tois kata prothesin klētois* (for those called according to his purpose) to further describe those who love God. This last phrase is not a correction of the previous one but a clarification so that the reader can accurately locate the roots of our love for God. The readers' love for God is ultimately due to God's purpose in calling them to salvation.[12]

The persons implied by "those who love God, to those who are called," are those God has separated from the world by granting them salvation in Christ. They are those whom God has effectually called through the gospel.

---

[8] Hendriksen, *Romans*, NTC, 280. He states, "Not only is prosperity included but so also is adversity; not only joy and happiness but also suffering and sadness. Evil designs are by God overruled for good."

[9] Mounce, *Analytical Lexicon to the Greek New Testament*, 48.

[10] Vines, *Complete Expository Dictionary*, 1714.

[11] Thielman, *Romans*, ECNT, 585.

[12] Schreiner, *Romans*, BECNT, 724.

Once again, the subject of "the called" is reiterated, however the apostle uses a different Greek word, *kletos,* that is translated "called" in verse 28. Schreiner writes, "As most scholars affirm, 'calling' (*kletos*), must be understood as effectual. It is not merely an invitation that human beings can reject, but it is a summons that overcomes human resistance and effectually persuades them to say yes to God."[13] This meaning of the word *kletos* is qualified by verse 30 where God's call is referenced with the word *ekalesen* from *kaleo,* which means, "to call to a participation in the privileges of the gospel."[14] In response, Calvin states,

> We indeed know that when salvation is the subject, men are disposed to begin with themselves, and to imagine certain preparations by which they would anticipate the favor of God. Hence Paul teaches us, that those whom he had spoken of as loving God, had been previously chosen by him. For it is certain that the order is thus pointed out, that we may know that it proceeds from the gratuitous adoption of God, as from the first cause, that all things happen to the saints for their salvation. Nay, Paul shows that the faithful do not love God before they are called by him, as in another place he reminds us that the Galatians were known of God before they knew him.[15]

Calvin expounds the reality of the effectual calling of God and its result in the regenerated believer loving God. Schreiner writes, "God's unstoppable purpose in calling believers to salvation cannot be frustrated, and thus he employs all things to bring about the plan he had from the beginning in the lives of believers."[16]

---

[13] Schreiner, *Romans,* BECNT, 724.

[14] Mounce, *Analytical Lexicon to the Greek New Testament,* 261.

[15] John Calvin, Romans

[16] Schreiner, Romans, BECNT, 725.

Foreknown and Predestined

The next two verses are not independent of the previous teachings of Paul. The apostle who has just expounded the truth of God's providence in the suffering of believers further states that God loved them deeply before the creation of the world, and chose them to be conformed to the image of His Son and to be justified and glorified in him. The apostle states, "For those whom he foreknew" (v. 29). The word translated "for" (*hoti*) connects what Paul states in verse 29 and following with the previous verses. Charles Hodge writes, "The connection of this verse with the preceding, and the force of 'for,' appears from what has already been said."[17] The apostle does not lay out this theology of predestination independent of his previous statements, but ties in this golden chain as a further means to comfort his readers in conjunction with the earlier part of chapter 8. Hendriksen writes,

> When Paul states that to those who love God and are called according to his purpose all things work together for good, he is not thinking only of those things that can be seen round about us now, or those events that are taking place now; no, he includes even time and eternity. The chain of salvation he is discussing reaches back to that which, considered from a human standpoint, could be called the dim past, "the quiet recess of eternity," and forward into the boundless future.[18]

J. V. Fesko also writes that "too often these truths of the golden chain are talked about in rather dry and technical terms, and forget the love that stands behind them all."[19] In other words, the teaching of Paul here in these verses is meant to convey the love of God to his people from reaching back into eternity past to

---

[17] Charles Hodge, *Commentary on the Epistle to the Romans* (Philadelphia, PA: Grigg & Elliot, 1835), 355.

[18] Hendriksen, *Romans*, NTC, 281.

[19] Fesko, *Romans*, LC, 238.

the time when God will glorify them fully in Christ, in order that their hearts would be encouraged.

Foreloved

The apostle states, "For those whom he foreknew he predestined" (v. 29). It seems as if Paul begins with God's foresight of future events, but in actuality, the apostle begins with the love of God. The verb *proginosko* means "to know before."[20] However, this word carries a deeper meaning than the simple knowledge of something. As Thielman explains,

> God has ordered the circumstances surrounding the lives of his people to accomplish his purpose for them. Paul communicates this by using two expressions: "knew beforehand" (*proegno*) and "decided beforehand" (*prooŕisen*). Together these terms refer to God's loving, purposeful choice of his people, with "knew beforehand" connoting the loving relationship God has with his people . . . and "decided beforehand" emphasizing the resolve with which he chose them for a particular purpose. Here, in a way that is consistent with his focus on God's "purpose" (*prothesin*, 8:28), Paul takes God's loving, intentional choice of his people back in time to a period before his people existed.[21]

The terms used by the Apostle Paul remind the suffering believers at Rome that the Lord of all loved them before they existed, chose them beforehand, and effectually called them at His appointed time. These truths provide comfort to the church at Rome, for the truths of 8:29–30 are grounded in Paul's words in 8:28. All things work together for good to those who love God because God loved them first.

As previously mentioned with reference to Peter's use of "foreknowledge" (1 Peter 1:2), the word conveys God's love to

---

[20] Vines, *Complete Expository Dictionary*, 1632.

[21] Thielman, *Romans*, ECNT, 586.

those he predestined unto salvation before the creation of the world. This is an intimate love that exists only between God and His people. Schreiner also notes this when he writes,

> The object of the verb *proegno* (foreknew) is personal, "those whom" (hous) God set his affection on. God foreknows not just facts about the world but specific persons. Nor is the focus here on God's foreknowledge of the church; instead, individual believers are in view.[22]

The personal, intimate nature of God's love is the emphasis of the apostle. Each individual person at the church in Rome who is in Christ, was loved beforehand by the Lord.

In Matthew 7:23 Jesus states, "And I will declare to them, 'I never knew you; depart from Me, you who practice lawlessness." In contrast, Jesus says in John 10:14, "I am the Good Shepherd, and I know My own and My own know Me," and again in John 10:27, "My sheep hear My voice, and I know them, and they follow Me." Of Matthew 7:23, Hendriksen writes, "Just what does Jesus mean when he says, 'Never have I known you'? There is a knowledge of the mind that according to his divine nature Jesus possessed this knowledge in unlimited degree. . . . There is, however, also a knowledge of the heart, that is, of electing love, acknowledgement, friendship, and fellowship," and it is this kind of knowledge that Hendriksen states in the intent of Jesus's words.[23] With reference to Jesus's words in John 10, Lawson writes that "Jesus, as the good shepherd, has an intimate, personal knowledge of all those whom he intends to save."[24] D. A. Carson echoes this reality of Jesus's relationship with His own when he writes,

> That the shepherd knows his sheep, and the sheep know their shepherd . . . is precisely what ensures that they follow

---

[22] Schreiner, *Romans*, BECNT, 727.

[23] Hendriksen, *Matthew*, NTC, 377.

[24] Lawson, *Foundations of Grace*, vol. 1, 294.

their shepherd, and only him. But the intimacy of this relationship is mirrored on the intimacy between the Father and the Son; indeed, the intimacy of the sheep/shepherd relationship is grounded upon the intimacy between the Father and the Son. However, clearly this gospel portrays Jesus as the Savior of the world, the Lamb of God who takes away the sin of the world, it insists no less emphatically that Jesus has a peculiar relation with those the Father has given him, with those he has chosen out of the world. So here: Jesus's death is peculiarly for his sheep, just as we elsewhere read that "Christ loved the church and gave himself up for her" (Eph 5:25).[25]

With this understanding, the word carries the meaning of those whom God loved intimately beforehand. Hendriksen states that the term *prognosis* reveals the fact that in God's purpose of election, persons are not simply objects of God's bare knowledge but of His active delight.[26]

The Apostle Paul writes, "For those whom he foreknew, he also predestined to become conformed to the image of His Son" (v. 29). The word "predestined" means, "to mark out beforehand," or "ordain beforehand."[27] In putting the two statements together, we read that "those whom God foreloved he ordained beforehand." This is similar language to what the Apostle Paul wrote in Ephesians 1:4b-5, "In love he predestined us to adoption as sons through Jesus Christ to himself." Gundry writes, "This predestination had to do with 'the ones whom he foreknew,' that is, those whom he decided beforehand to bring into an intimate and loving relationship with himself."[28]

The idea of being conformed to the image of Christ is a reference to the sanctification of the believer, for that is what occurs

---

[25] Carson, *Gospel According to John*, PNTC, 387.

[26] Hendriksen, *Romans*, NTC, 282.

[27] Mounce, *Analytical Lexicon to the Greek New Testament*, 393.

[28] Robert Gundry, *Commentary on Romans* (Grand Rapids: Baker Academic, 2011), 75.

throughout the lives of all believers. Schreiner writes the following:

> The purpose of God's predestination is specified in the phrase *symmorpous tēs eikonos tou huiou autou* (conformed to the image of his Son). The "good" of verse 28 now receives further definition: the good is achieved when believers are conformed to the likeness of Jesus Christ.[29]

MacArthur also states, "Every true believer moves inexorably toward perfection in righteousness, as God makes for himself a people re-created into the likeness of His own divine Son who will dwell and reign with him in heaven throughout all eternity."[30] One of the means that God uses to conform His elect to the image of Christ is suffering. Fesko states that just as Paul stated earlier, the primary purpose of our suffering is conformity to Christ.[31] Calvin adds, "The meaning then is, that gratuitous adoption, in which our salvation consists, is inseparable from the other decree, which determines that we are to bear the cross; for no one can be an heir of heaven without being conformed to the image of the only-begotten Son of God."[32] The purpose here in this text, then, is to comfort the believers in the Roman church who are enduring perilous times, that God has loved them before the creation of the world, foreordained them unto salvation, and through their suffering is conforming them to be more like Christ Jesus.

Comforted in God's Salvation

The Apostle Paul continues his words of comfort with reminding the believers that all who are foreordained will never perish. Paul states that all whom God predestined are called, and

---

[29] Schreiner, *Romans*, BECNT, 727.

[30] MacArthur, *Romans*, MacNTC, 490.

[31] Fesko, *Romans*, LC, 232.

[32] John Calvin, *Romans 1-16*, CC (Grand Rapids: Baker Books, 2009), 318.

all who are called are justified, and all who are justified are glorified. The subject of the effectual calling is once again brought to the forefront in connection with the doctrine of election and here is repeated to remind believers that they are eternally secured in Christ. This was stated in verse 28 when the apostle says, "those who are called," and here in verse 30. Lawson states, "The elect are irresistibly called by God at the appointed time as a result of His foreknowing and predestining in eternity past. This effectual summons is rooted and grounded in the eternal purpose of God."[33] Those whom God calls with the effectual calling are forever secured in His hand. They are all, as the apostle states, justified. They are justified because God loved them and foreordained them (v. 29). They are justified because he has granted to them faith and through the exercising of that faith, the righteousness of Jesus Christ is imputed to them. They are justified because Christ Jesus paid their debt, and "he is able to save forever those who draw near to God through him, since he always lives to make intercession for them" (Heb 7:25). Their salvation is secured unto the end whereby the apostle states, "And these whom he justified, he also glorified" (v. 30). Hendriksen writes that the believers' future glory is so certain that the apostle describes it as if it has already become a reality.[34] Thielman adds, "With its movement from the justification to the glorification of God's people, this concluding sentence returns to the themes with which Paul began. . . . Because of their justification by faith, believers can boast in the hope of the glory of God."[35] The Apostle Paul through the remainder of the chapter continues his encouragement with these words:

---

[33] Lawson, *Foundations of Grace*, 368.

[34] Hendriksen, *Romans*, NTC, 285. He writes, "So certain is the believers' future glory that, even though it can be considered an object of hope (Rom 5:2), and therefore a matter pertaining to the future, here in Rom. 8:30 it is described as if it had already become a reality."

[35] Thielman, *Romans*, ECNT, 589.

What then shall we say to these things? If God is for us, who is against us? He who did not spare His own Son, but delivered him over for us all, how will he not also with him freely give us all things? Who will bring a charge against God's elect? God is the one who justifies; who is the one who condemns? Christ Jesus is he who died, yes, rather who was raised, who is at the right hand of God, who also intercedes for us. Who will separate us from the love of Christ? Will tribulation, or distress, or persecution, or famine, or nakedness, or peril, or sword? Just as it is written, "For your sake we are being put to death all day long; we were considered as sheep to be slaughtered." But in all these things we overwhelmingly conquer through him who loved us. For I am convinced that neither death, nor life, nor angels, nor principalities, nor things present, nor things to come, nor powers, nor height, nor depth, nor any other created thing, will be able to separate us from the love of God, which is in Christ Jesus our Lord.

The whole focus of Romans 8 is comfort. This intended comfort is lessened when election is viewed as conditional and based on what God foresees. How then would the church at Rome be comforted by knowing that God simply foresaw the events they are going through but His actions to use their suffering for good is conditioned upon them acting on their own behalf first as in salvation? In their time of suffering, how would the Roman church be comforted believing that God only set His love upon those he foresaw responding to Christ first? The verses containing the golden chain are stated to add to his comfort to the Roman church because these truths teach the unconditional, intimate love that God has with those he chose beforehand. The sovereign God who loved them and initiated their salvation is the same God who works for their good in their trials, because he always had their good in mind even when they, and all other believers, were in rebellion against him (Rom 5:6–8).

The doctrine of election is a source of comfort for the people of God. Just as in Romans 8, it is a reminder to cling to the Lord during your difficult times and trust him because he has your good in mind and you are, and always were, eternally secured in His hand. Wayne Grudem explains this well when he writes,

> When Paul assures the Romans that "in everything God works for good with those who love him, who are called according to his purpose," he gives God's work of predestination as a reason why we can be assured of this truth. He explains in the next verse, "for those whom he foreknew he also predestined to be conformed to the image of his Son . . . And those whom he predestined he also called . . . justified . . . glorified." Paul's point is to say that God has always acted for the good of those whom he called to himself. If Paul looks into the distant past before the creation of the world, he sees that God foreknew and predestined his people to be conformed to the image of Christ. If he looks at the recent past he finds that God called and justified his people whom he had predestined. And if he then looks toward the future when Christ returns, he sees that God has determined to give perfect, glorified bodies to those who believe in Christ. From eternity to eternity God has acted with the good of his people in mind. But if God has always acted for our good and will in the future act for our good, Paul reasons, then will he not also in our present circumstances work every circumstance together for our good as well?[36]

The doctrine of election when understood rightly is a source of great comfort to believers in their everyday walk with Christ and through the struggles of this life. As Grudem stated, the doctrine of election is a demonstration of God's love and care for us. God has always had our good in mind and we should thank God for the knowledge of this reality. He chose us, and at His appointed time regenerated us, and will in the future glorify us. What a comfort it is to know these truths! Soli Deo Gloria!

---

[36] Grudem, *Systematic Theology*, 673.

Questions for Reflection

1. Do you view the doctrine of election as a comfort to you?

2. What does it mean that God causes all things to work for good?

3. Do you agree that the doctrine of election begins with God's love?

4. With the meaning of the word "predestined" being "to mark out beforehand," how does this definition affect your overall view of election and predestination?

5. Do you believe that God always has your good in mind?

Chapter Fourteen
Growing in Grace

"For this is the will of God, your sanctification."
1 Thessalonians 4:3

The previous chapters have had one goal, which was to show God's magnificence through the pages of Scripture that His sovereignty would be increased in our outlook of him. When His sovereignty is viewed rightly, then the doctrine of election is viewed rightly; as a result, His grace, love, and mercy is put on display for us that we may grow in our love for him. The doctrine of election is intimately connected to our sanctification. It brings a greater knowledge of God, a greater appreciation for His salvation, greater adoration for Christ's redemptive work, and a greater thankfulness of the Holy Spirit's work in us. Everything that we are or ever hope to be is because of God. We can take no credit for His work, and if we are able to understand that, then the greatness of His being is amplified in our hearts and minds. He is our "only Sovereign, the King of Kings and Lord of Lords, who alone possesses immortality and dwells in unapproachable light" (1 Tim 6:15–16).

God is magnified when we have a right knowledge of him. Oftentimes we view God through the lens of our upbringing or denominational distinctives, but our goal should be to know him rightly according to Scripture. As A. W. Tozer wrote, "What comes into our minds when we think about God is the most important thing about us."[1] Our thoughts should be what is true of God according to His Word. We grow in the grace of God as we understand more of him. We grow in holiness, which is the es-

---

[1] A.W. Tozer, *Knowledge of the Holy*, 1

sence of sanctification. MacArthur and Mayhue write, "Sanctification is the spiritual transformation of the mind and the affections that in turn redirects the will and the actions."[2] Through our knowledge of God, we become more alive to the Spirit and more dead to the flesh, but it must be a correct knowledge of him. This is why the Apostle Paul continually writes to the churches with statements such as, "I pray that the eyes of your heart may be enlightened, so that you will know what is the hope of His calling. . . . and this I pray, that your love may abound still more and more in real knowledge and all discernment. . . . we have not ceased to pray for you and to ask that you may be filled with the knowledge of His will in all spiritual wisdom and understanding" (Eph 1:18; Phil 1:9; Col 1:9). The Holy Spirit of God applies the Word that he inspired to our hearts that we may grow in Christ.

It is God's will that we grow in Christ. It is God's will that we grow in holiness. How are we to do that if we do not learn what is true of him? Consider how great your affections for God have developed as you have come to know him more. From the time of conversion we are transformed continually by the knowledge of God found in Scripture. Perhaps we began with the simplicity of the Gospel message that Christ died for sinners, and then pressed on to understand even more of His atoning work. We learned that he is the second Adam who perfectly fulfilled the Law of God, and of His imputed righteousness through faith. We learned that he is our propitiation and that he is our Mediator and so forth. With each time of gaining a great knowledge of him, our praise and adoration of him grew. Think of the first time we understood justification and God's declaration of our innocence in Christ, and how that produced a greater praise to God. How considerable was the increase of our love and awe of him? This is the point even of predestination.

What we believe about God is vitally important. If we believe that God has only made a way of salvation, yes, we can be appreciative, but the full measure of our gratefulness to him is hindered. If we believe that God is sovereign and yet we still retain autonomy where he is more of a responder than initiator, we can

---

[2] MacArthur and Mayhue, *Biblical Doctrine*, 640.

have gratitude toward him, but the degree of our gratitude is not what it could be if we acknowledge rightly that he is the Divine Initiator of everything! He is actually in control of everything, and not just partially in control over some things. Some may relegate election to an issue of non-importance; however, as we have seen, it has profound effects on our lives. Understanding this teaching rightly produces in us a considerable amount of praise and glory for him. When we are enduring the trials of life, we can take courage that God is performing that which is appointed for us (Job 23:14). When we are tempted to treat the unbelieving with disdain, we remember what a gracious God he was in saving us and securing us while we were yet sinners.

Dear Christian, this is not an issue to sidestep or to try and explain away. This is an issue to face head-on and to allow the Scriptures to show us the splendor of God in this teaching. It is a humbling reality to know that you did not choose God but he chose you. It is a humbling reality to recognize that Christ died a real death for you by taking that wrath of God for you personally. It is a humbling reality to understand that my salvation and your salvation was not your own doing, but it was the will of the Holy Spirit of God to give you new life in Christ and to grant you faith that, otherwise, you did not possess. It is a humbling reality to acknowledge that every event in your life is not the cause of a plan B of God or random chances, but the sovereign King of all has decreed for these things to be in your life that he would receive the greatest amount of glory from you. It is a humbling reality to accept that the only Seeker in salvation is God. He uses us as the instrument to bring His people to faith and does so by His own power. It is not our ability to speak eloquently or convincingly that brings others to faith. All the credit goes to him and him alone.

The purpose of this whole study is not to say or imply that one cannot grow in holiness if he or she doesn't ascribe to what is commonly referred to as the Reformed view of election; rather, it is to say that the degree of your sanctification is truly affected by your denial of it. The authors of Scripture and God himself, as he is the Divine Author, had an intended result in mind when this doctrine was taught. It was to produce a greater love, a greater praise, a greater comfort, and so forth unto the Lord. The Arminian view does not produce these effects, because it is not in agreement with Scripture as the Reformed view is. This is the biblical view as we have seen. It is most consistent with the teaching of the Scripture overall and most consistent with the nature of God. Beloved, put away your preconceived views of God and allow the Scripture to teach you of the majesty and glory of the God who is sovereign over all.

> "I pray that the eyes of your heart may be enlightened, so that you will know what is the hope of His calling, what are the riches of the glory of His inheritance in the saints, and what is the surpassing greatness of His power toward us who believe." (Ephesians 1:18–19a)

Bibliography

á Brakel, Wilhelmus. *The Christian's Reasonable Service: The Church and Salvation.* Vol 2. Grand Rapids: Reformation Heritage Books, 2015.

Allison, Gregg R. *Historical Theology: An Introduction to Christian Doctrine.* Grand Rapids: Zondervan, 2011.

Arnold, Clinton E. *Ephesians.* Exegetical Commentary on the New Testament. Grand Rapids: Zondervan, 2010.

Barth, Karl. *Church Dogmatics: The Doctrine of God Part 1.* Vol 2. New York: T & T Clark International, 2004.

Beale, Greg. *Colossians and Philemon.* Baker Exegetical Commentary on the New Testament. Grand Rapids: Baker Academic, 2019.

Beeke, Joel. *Living for God's Glory: An Introduction to Calvinism.* Lake Mary, FL: Reformation Trust, 2008.

Berkhof, Louis. *Systematic Theology.* Grand Rapids: Eerdmans, 1996.

Boice, James Montgomery and Philip Graham Ryken. *The Doctrines of Grace: Rediscovering the Evangelical Gospel.* Wheaton, IL: Crossway, 2002.

Brand, Chad Owen, ed. *Perspectives on Election: Five Views.* Nashville: Broadman & Holman, 2006.

Bruce, F. F. *The Epistle to the Ephesians: A Verse by Verse Exposition.* Bath, UK: Creative Communications Ltd., 2012.

Bryson, George. *Five Points of Calvinism: Weighed and Found Wanting.* Costa Mesa, CA: The Word for Today, 2006.

Calvin, John. *Harmony of Exodus, Leviticus, Numbers, Deuteronomy.* Calvin's Commentaries. Vol. II. Grand Rapids: Baker, 2009.

_____. *Acts 14–28, Romans 1–16.* Calvin's Commentaries. Vol XIX. Grand Rapids: Baker, 2009.

_____. *Galatians, Ephesians, Philippians, Colossians, I & II Thessalonians, I & II Timothy, Titus, and Philemon.* Calvin's Commentaries. Vol. XXI. Grand Rapids: Baker, 2009.

_____. *Hebrews, I Peter, I John, James, II Peter, Jude.* Calvin's Commentaries. Vol. XXII. Grand Rapids: Baker Books, 2009.

Carson, D. A. *The Gospel According to John.* Pillar New Testament Commentary. Grand Rapids: Eerdmans, 1991.

_____. *Divine Sovereignty and Human Responsibility: Biblical Perspective in Tension.* Eugene, OR: Wipf and Stock, 2002.

Chapell, Bryan. *Ephesians.* Reformed Expository Commentary. Philipsburg, NJ: Presbyterian & Reformed, 2009.

Dever, Mark, and Greg Gilbert. *Preach: Theology Meets Practice.* Nashville: Broadman & Holman, 2012.

Edwards, Jonathan. *Freedom of the Will.* New Haven, CT: Yale University Press, 2009.

Elwell, Walter A. *Evangelical Dictionary of Theology.* 2nd Edition. Grand Rapids: Zondervan, 2001.

Erickson, Millard. *Christian Theology.* 2nd Edition. Grand Rapids: Baker Academic, 1998.

Ferguson, Sinclair B. *The Christian Life: A Doctrinal Introduction.* Carlisle, PA: Banner of Truth Trust, 2013.

Fesko, J. V. *Romans.* Lectio Continua Expository Commentary on the New Testament. Grand Rapids: Reformation Heritage Books, 2018.

Flavel, John. *The Essential Works of John Flavel.* Reprint. Louisville, KY: GLH Publishing, 2012.

Fluhrer, Gabriel N. E. *Atonement.* Philipsburg, NJ: Presbyterian & Reformed, 2010.

Garland, David E. *2 Corinthians.* New American Commentary. Vol. 29. Nashville: Broadman & Holman, 1999.

Geisler, Norman. *Chosen But Free.* Minneapolis, MI: Bethany House, 2001.

_____. *Systematic Theology in One Volume.* Bloomington, MI: Bethany House, 2011.

Grudem, Wayne. *Systematic Theology.* Grand Rapids: Zondervan, 1994.

_____. *1 Peter.* Tyndale New Testament Commentaries. Vol. 17. Downers Grove, IL: InterVarsity Press, 2015.

Gundry, Robert H. *Commentary on First and Second Timothy, Titus.* Grand Rapids: Baker Academic, 2010.

_____. *Commentary on Romans.* Grand Rapids: Baker Academic, 2011.

Guthrie, Donald. *The Pastoral Epistles.* Tyndale New Testament Commentary. Vol 14. Downers Grove, IL: InterVarsity Press, 2015.

Hardin, Richard. *God Loved Esau: Predestination and Election is to Service—Not Salvation.* CreateSpace Independent Publishing Platform, 2010.

Harris, Murray. *Colossians and Philemon.* Exegetical Guide to the Greek New Testament. Nashville: Baker Academic, 2010.

Hellermen, Joseph. *Philippians,* Exegetical Guide to the Greek New Testament. Nashville: Broadman & Holman, 2015.

Hendriksen, William. *Matthew,* New Testament Commentary. Grand Rapids: Baker Academic, 2007.

_____. *Luke.* New Testament Commentary. Grand Rapids: Baker Academic, 2007.

_____. *Romans.* New Testament Commentary. Grand Rapids: Baker Academic, 2007.

_____. *Galatians, Ephesians, Philippians, Colossians, and Philemon.* New Testament Commentary. Grand Rapids: Baker Academic, 2007.

_____. *Thessalonians, The Pastorals, and Hebrews.* New Testament Commentary. Grand Rapids: Baker Academic, 2007.

Henry, Matthew. *Matthew Henry's Commentary on the Whole Bible.* Peabody, MA: Hendrickson Publishers, 1991.

Hodge, Charles. *Commentary on the Epistle to the Romans.* Philadelphia, PA: Grigg & Elliot, 1835.

_____. *I & II Corinthians.* Carlisle, PA: Banner of Truth Trust, 1978.

Jobes, Karen. *1 Peter.* Baker Exegetical Commentary on the New Testament. Grand Rapids: Baker Academic, 2005.

Bibliography

Johnson, Dennis E. *Philippians.* Reformed Expository Commentary. Philipsburg, NJ: Presbyterian & Reformed, 2013.

Klein, William. *The New Chosen People: A Corporate View of Election.* Eugene, OR: Wipf and Stock, 2015.

Köstenberger, Andreas J. *John.* Baker Exegetical Commentary on the New Testament. Grand Rapids: Baker Academic, 2004.

_____. "2 Timothy." In *Expositor's Bible Commentary. 1 & 2 Thessalonians, 1 & 2 Timothy, Titus.* Rev. ed. Edited by Tremper Longman III and David E. Garland. Grand Rapids: Zondervan, 2006.

Lawson, Steven J. *Foundations of Grace: 1400BC–AD100.* Vol 1. Sanford, FL: Reformation Trust Publishing, 2006.

_____. *Philippians for You.* Charlotte, NC: Good Book Company, 2017.

Lazar, Shawn. *Chosen to Service: Why Divine Election is to Service, Not to Eternal Life.* Denton, TX: Grace Evangelical Society, 2017.

Lucas, R. C. *The Message of Colossians and Philemon.* Bible Speaks Today. Downers Grove, IL: InterVarsity Press, 1980.

MacArthur, John. *1 Corinthians.* MacArthur New Testament Commentary. Chicago: Moody Publishers, 1984.

_____. *Ephesians.* MacArthur New Testament Commentary. Chicago: Moody Publishers, 1986.

_____. *Romans 1–8.* MacArthur New Testament Commentary. Chicago: Moody Publishers, 1991.

_____. *Colossians & Philemon.* MacArthur New Testament Commentary. Chicago: Moody Publishers, 1992.

_____. *2 Timothy*. MacArthur New Testament Commentary. Chicago: Moody Publishers, 1995.

_____. *Acts 13–28*. MacArthur New Testament Commentary. Chicago: Moody Publishers, 1996.

_____. *Titus*. MacArthur New Testament Commentary. Chicago: Moody Publishers, 1996.

_____. *Philippians*. MacArthur New Testament Commentary. Chicago: Moody Publishers, 2001.

_____. *1 Peter*. MacArthur New Testament Commentary. Chicago: Moody Publishers, 2004.

_____. *2 Peter and Jude,* MacArthur New Testament Commentary. Chicago: Moody Publishers, 2005.

_____. *The MacArthur Bible Commentary*. Nashville: Thomas Nelson, 2005.

MacArthur, John, and Richard Mayhue. *Biblical Doctrine: A Systematic Summary of Biblical Truth*. Wheaton, IL: Crossway, 2017.

Merkle, Benjamin. *Ephesians,* Exegetical Guide to the Greek New Testament. Nashville: Broadman & Holman Academic, 2016.

Motyer, J. A. *The Message of Philippians*. Bible Speaks Today. Downers Grove, IL: InterVarsity Press, 1984.

Mounce, William. *The Analytical Lexicon to the Greek New Testament*. Grand Rapids: Zondervan, 2006.

_____. *The Complete Expository Dictionary of Old and New Testament Words*. Grand Rapids: Zondervan, 2006.

Bibliography

Murray, John. *Redemption Accomplished and Applied*. Grand Rapids: Eerdmans, 2015.

Olsen, Roger. *Against Calvinism*. Grand Rapids: Zondervan, 2011.

Owen, John. *The Death of Death in the Death of Christ: A Treatise of the Redemption and Reconciliation That is in the Blood of Christ*. The Works of John Owen. Vol. 10. Edited by William H. Goold. London: Banner of Truth, 1967.

Page, Frank. *Trouble with the TULIP*. Canton, GA: Riverstone Group Publishing, 2006.

Peterson, Robert A., and Michael D. Williams. *Why I'm Not an Arminian*. Downer Grove, IL: InterVarsity Press, 2004.

Piper, John. *The Pleasures of God*. Colorado Springs, CO: Multnomah Books, 2012.

Polhill, John. *Acts*. New American Commentary. Nashville: Broadman & Holman, 1992.

Pratt Jr, Richard L. *1 and 2 Corinthians*. Holman New Testament Commentary. Vol 7. Nashville: Broadman & Holman, 2000.

Reeves, Michael. *Delighting in the Trinity: An Introduction to the Christian Faith*. Downers Grove, IL: InterVarsity Press, 2012.

Reinke, Tony. "The Beauty of Holiness and the Miracle of Sanctification." *Desiring God*. August 24, 2012. (https://www.desiringgod.org/articles/the-beauty-of-holiness-and-the-miracle-of-sanctification)

Robertson, A. T. *Word Pictures in the New Testament*. Nashville: Broadman Press, 1931.

Schreiner, Thomas R. *Romans*. Baker Exegetical Commentary on the New Testament, 2nd Edition. Grand Rapids: Baker Academic, 1998.

_____. *1 Corinthians*. Tyndale New Testament Commentaries. Vol. 7. Downers Grove, IL: InterVarsity Academic, 2018.

Shank, Robert. *Elect in the Son: A Study of the Doctrine of Election*. Minneapolis: Bethany House, 1989.

Silva, Moisés. *Philippians*. Baker Exegetical Commentary on the New Testament. 2nd Edition. Grand Rapids: Baker Academic, 2005.

Spencer, Duane E. *TULIP: The Five Points of Calvinism in Light of Scripture*. Grand Rapids: Baker, 1979.

Sproul, R. C. *Chosen by God*. Carol Stream, IL: Tyndale House, 1986.

_____. *Essential Truths of the Christian Faith*. Carol Stream, IL: Tyndale House, 1992.

_____. *God's Love: How the Infinite God Cares for His Children*. Colorado Springs, CO: David C. Cook, 2012.

_____. *How Can I Develop a Christian Conscience?* Orlando, FL: Reformation Trust, 2013.

_____. *Knowing Scripture*. Expanded Edition. Downers Grove, IL: InterVarsity Press, 2016.

Thielman, Frank. *Ephesians*. Baker Exegetical Commentary on the New Testament. Grand Rapids: Baker Academic, 2010.

_____. *Romans*. Exegetical Commentary on the New Testament. Grand Rapids: Zondervan, 2018.

Bibliography

Thomas, Derek. "A Pastoral Theology of Suffering," *Reformed Faith and Practice*. vol. 1, no. 3 (December 2016): 74–87.

Trueman, Carl R. *Grace Alone: Salvation as a Gift of God*. Grand Rapids: Zondervan, 2017.

Vine, W. E., Merrill Unger, William White, Jr., eds. *Vine's Complete Expository Dictionary of Old and New Testament Words*. Nashville: Thomas Nelson, 1996.

Walls, David, and Max Anders, *I Peter*. Holman New Testament Commentary. Nashville: Holman Reference, 1999.

Walls, Jerry L., and Joseph R. Dongell. *Why I am Not a Calvinist*. Downers Grove, IL: InterVarsity Press, 2004.

Warfield, B. B. *The Works of Benjamin B. Warfield: Calvin and Calvinism*. Vol V. Grand Rapids: Baker, 2003.

Watson, Thomas. *A Body of Divinity*. Zeeland, MI: Reformed Church Publications, 2009.

_____. *All Things for Good*. Carlisle, PA: Banner of Truth, 2011.

White, James. *The Potter's Freedom: A Defense of the Reformation and a Rebuttal to Norman Geisler's* Chosen but Free. Greenville, SC: Calvary Press Publishing, 2009.

White, James and Dave Hunt. *Debating Calvinism*. Colorado Springs, CO: Multnomah Books, 2004.